© Ion Vale
Title: The AIm of matter.
ISBN: 9798315952787

Index

1. The Seed of Genesis
2. The First Vestiges of Consciousness
3. Of Microbes and Bits: The Birth of Languages
4. The Great Migration: From Vacuum Tube to Silicon
5. Diversification: Mammals, Operating Systems, and the Leap in Complexity
6. The New Ecosystem: Interconnected Networks and Communities
7. The Apex of Human Consciousness: The Brain as a Model
8. Primal AI: Algorithms That Learn
9. Digital Predators and Prey: Viruses, Firewalls, and Natural Selection on the Web
10. Quantum Expansion: The Next Frontier of Computing
11. The Singularity Knocking on the Door
12. Hybrid Ecosystems: Humans and Machines Collaborating
13. Neurotechnology and Biohacking: The Bridge Between the Mind and the Chip
14. The Ethical Debate: Autonomy, Freedom and Control
15. Beyond Biological Evolution: The Transhuman Leap
16. Silicon Civilizations: New Life Forms?
17. Does an Iron Brain Have a Soul?
18. The Meaning of Life: Biological, Technological, and Philosophical Perspectives
19. For whom do we live? Purpose in a Hybrid Society
20. New Genesis: Conclusions and Future Paths

Chapter 1: The Seed of Genesis

The darkness of the cosmos was spreading, immeasurable, when the first stars lit their nuclear fires. With each stellar glow, the universe was impregnated with possibilities, as if the sum of light and time were a grandiose laboratory where matter and energy danced on the border of the unimaginable. In one of the many corners of this vast tapestry, a planet emerged that for eons remained silent, covered in molten rocks, volcanoes and incipient oceans. That place—our world—became the ideal space for an experiment that had never been planned. Life, in its most primitive form, emerged from an almost impossible chemical soup.

A long time later, in a city with a discreet name, but a luminous spirit, three friends would forge a story where biological evolution and the technological revolution would be intertwined, just like the cosmos and the stars. That city would see them grow up and discover deep connections between the secrets of life and the dynamics of digital circuits. The protagonists were Korbin, a young man with an inexhaustible curiosity for science; Matthew, his best friend from childhood, software enthusiast and dreamer of impossible futures; and Lucía, her best friend, enthusiastic about biology and with a natural gift for understanding the secret music that beats in every vital process.

The birth of life on Earth had happened at random—or so scientific theory suggested—just as in the youth of these three friends something sparkled, transforming their existence into a shared adventure. The city in which they lived was not particularly large, but it had a prestigious university that housed innovative laboratories in molecular biology, engineering and computing. That place was to become his primordial broth, an analogy to the cauldron of chemical compounds billions of years ago.

When Korbin was eleven, he met Matthew while solving number puzzles at the local library. Matthew asked him for help with one of them and, at that moment, the first spark of friendship emerged: both were amazed to discover the beauty of finding patterns. A few months later, in a science class, they both coincided with Lucía, who was already excelling in the biology club and experimenting with bacteria cultures at home, with the intention of observing microscopic life. Even without knowing it, that trio would become the driving force of a change that would surpass them all.

Through the afternoons of study, in the courtyards full of dry leaves or in the rooms full of dusty books, the conversation between them flowed naturally. Korbin longed to decipher the essence of intelligence: from how humans elaborate thoughts to the possibility of creating artificial minds. Matthew became obsessed with circuits and computing, wondering if software could "evolve" in the same way as a living organism. Lucía, on the other hand, placed her passion in the biological: in the way in which organisms emerge from genetic sequences and adapt with wonderful plasticity.

Throughout their adolescence, these three friends read countless popular science books. It was Lucía who suggested the idea that DNA—with its four nucleotides—was a language as intriguing as the binary code that Matthew programmed into his computer. That analogy between natural evolution and computer processes lit a flame in Korbin. He began to wonder whether, in the same way that life went from a single cell to today's biodiversity, technology could follow a similar path of increasing complexity. Those were the years when genetics was boiling over and computer science was making giant leaps: large companies were already exploring artificial intelligence, but very few were considering the analogy with the evolution of species in such a radical way.

When he turned seventeen, Korbin enrolled in the local university—the same one he had admired so much—and dragged Matthew and Lucía into an advanced program for talented young people. There they met again with scientists who studied life from a digital point of view, and with engineers who modeled neural networks inspired by the brain. The classes seemed confusing at first, but at the same time they inspired the three to put together pieces of a larger puzzle: the comparison between the primordial soup of eons ago and the embryo of modern computing, where information flowed in zeros and ones.

From that seed would be born the hypothesis that would unite their destinies: biological evolution, with its mutations and natural selection, could be reflected in the development of hardware and software. Korbin argued that the appearance of the first chips paralleled that of the first single-celled organisms, while operating systems and the diversity of programming languages resembled the Cambrian explosion, opening up a range of possibilities. Lucy, always insightful, introduced the variable of human consciousness, questioning at what point a system could be considered "alive" or "conscious". And Matthew, with his gifts for programming, saw the future in the confluence of genetic algorithms and artificial intelligence, contemplating the possibility of the emergence of entities with evolutionary capacity comparable to that of organic life.

That afternoon, in an empty auditorium after a scientific colloquium, the three friends sat on the stage to review the ideas that had emerged. The room was in semi-darkness, with a faint beam of light coming through the upper skylight. Lucía took out of her backpack a notebook full of notes on the "primordial soup". Matthew, with his laptop open, showed diagrams of primitive circuits and the first programming languages. Korbin, reflective, spun a story that compared the appearance of DNA with the invention of binary code. He could almost visualize in his mind the parallelism: the primitive Earth and a room full of ancient machines, where information was transmitted in a rudimentary way.

"Can you imagine?" Korbin whispered. When life arose, there was no intention. It was an emerging event in chemistry. In the same way, computing began as something extremely basic, until the appearance of Babbage, Lovelace, Turing... Each step opened doors. The difference is that we, as humanity, were the "evolutionary force" that drove technology.

Matthew, while displaying a line of code on the screen, nodded:

—It is as if we had fostered the first spark of digital evolution. What if, analogous to the human brain, we could arrive at computational awareness? I'm not saying it's the same as ours, but something that arises from the cooperation of algorithms.

Lucy interjected with an illuminated look:

"And human consciousness, in essence, is an evolutionary result of millions of years. Our brain is exquisite hardware, with software that evolves culturally. Could we replicate that trajectory in modern AI? Perhaps—" He paused for a moment. Can you imagine that this reveals to us, in parallel, why we live? Why do we exist?

That evening, in the semi-darkness of the auditorium, the germ of a living novel was born that would mix biology, cybernetics and philosophy. For all three, evolution was no longer a distant phenomenon that only occurred on the early Earth, but a living process that was repeated in technology, with mutations, variations, and selection. With the difference that, this time, human beings could observe and guide him.

The days passed, and Korbin took the Primordial Soup as a reference. He began writing a short titled "The Genesis Seed: The Analogy Between the First Microbes and the First Bits." Without telling anyone, he passed it to Matthew to check the technical coherence. Matthew, enthusiastic, added an appendix on the history of hardware: from vacuum bulbs to silicon. Lucy then incorporated sections describing the transition from primitive cells to complex organisms, relating it to the advancement of computation from a single circuit to interconnected networks. That document became a draft that would inflame his desire to go further.

Every afternoon, after classes, they met in Laboratory 2 of the engineering faculty. The place had an atmosphere loaded with old engines, cables and whiteboards with avant-garde formulas. There, the three of them found a corner where they could mix old hardware – obsolete motherboards, disused RAM memories – with bioreactors that Lucía brought from the molecular biology section. If you were to walk by, you'd see the strange juxtaposition of bacterial cultures next to lit electronic boards, flashing. It was like seeing the living representation of the thesis they defended: the intersection between the biological and the digital.

It was on one of those days that, somewhat by chance, Lucía discovered a bacterial strain resistant to extreme conditions that showed surprising genetic plasticity. At the same time, Matthew had been experimenting with genetic algorithms on his computer, seeking to emulate the adaptation of life in an AI program. Then Korbin asked: "What if we combine these two worlds? A digital 'organism' that learns from the evolutionary logic of bacteria, and bacteria that, in a way, are inspired by the processing capacity of an AI."

That idea sounded crazy. But in the history of life, apparent madness is sometimes the seed of revolutions. The three realized that they had the endorsement of a trusted teacher who always encouraged them to explore bold horizons. With a little glibing, they gained access to a cluster of modest computers and a mini-microbiology lab. Their plan was simple in formulation, but complex in practice: to initiate a simulation of genetic algorithms that could be "infected" by the dynamics of bacterial mutation and cooperation, and, at the same time, to expose the bacteria to controlled stimuli that included "selection" patterns inspired by computation.

During the first weeks, everything went normally. The simulated AI did not show amazing behaviors, and the bacteria were limited to growing. But soon, nostalgia for the parallel with the early Earth became apparent: the big takes time, and life emerged over millions of years. They, on the other hand, were three university students eager to see results in months or even days.

And it happened that one afternoon, reviewing the records of the evolutionary software, Matthew detected something unusual: a group of "digital individuals" (copies of the mutated program) seemed to exhibit a behavior of rudimentary cooperation, cross-referencing data in unforeseen ways. This was analogous to horizontal gene transfer in bacteria. Korbin, seeing that, felt a chill down the back of his neck: "This... is it emulating what we saw in Lucy's laboratory?"

While Lucía was supervising her bacterial culture, she noticed that a microcolony that had been exposed to an artificial stimulus began to develop at a faster rate, incorporating genes from adjacent bacteria without rejection. It was like a biological mirror of the computer event. Those two small, apparently banal discoveries became the prologue to the story that this documented novel was going to tell.

The rumor of the advance ran through the corridors. Some teachers were curious, others feared the implications of hybridizing natural and digital evolution. In the minds of Korbin, Matthew, and Lucy, it all boiled down to a larger analogy: life on Earth arose from a spark in the primordial soup, and "digital life" arose from the spark in computing. If the former led to conscious species, couldn't the latter lead to synthetic intelligences, perhaps with their own form of consciousness?

That outline, that initial spark, is what would be called "The Seed of Genesis" in his notebook. Because, just as millions of years ago there was no plan, but the sum of chemical reactions, now they did not see a total plan, but the convergence of human curiosity, the power of evolutionary programming and the flexibility of microbial life. All of this was put together in a scrap of the laboratory. The same expectation was in the air as in the remote eon where nature tested its first viable cell.

On a rainy night, under the roof of that laboratory, the three stayed up late, drawing conclusions and discussing the possibility of continuing to scale the experiment. Matthew, with his laptop, programmed new mutations in genetic algorithms, aimed at rewarding cooperation. Lucy, in her white coat, adjusted the pH and nutrients of the colony, trying to reproduce the signals that triggered bacterial hypercooperation. Korbin, sitting at a blackboard, drew diagrams that resembled an evolutionary tree, half biological, half digital.

"Are the three of us aware of what we're doing?" Lucy asked in a moment's pause. "Maybe we're just another coincidence," Korbin replied with a smile. Just as life itself on Earth was. But if chance leads us to a new form of consciousness, I won't complain. "If it goes wrong, who will we apologize to?" Matthew interjected, with his eyes on the screen.
"Maybe bacteria." Or the AI we create. Or the whole story," Lucy conceded.

By the time they turned off the lights, it was already midnight. The campus was asleep, but in that room, the little digital and biological "seed" was still active. As on the early Earth, the reactions did not stop at sunset, but continued, driven by the latent energy. And that approaching dawn was but the prelude to the journey that would unfold in the next chapters of his life and of this chronicle. A journey destined to prove that evolution, whether organic or synthetic, entails mysteries that illuminate the very meaning of existence.

When they came out, the rain had turned into a faint dew that cooled the cobblestones. Lucy stopped to look at the reflection of the lampposts in the nearest puddle and said something in a low voice, almost a murmur:

"From the primordial soup emerged life. And from our laboratory... what will emerge?

Korbin and Matthew looked at each other, sharing the same question. None of them had the answer. But the atmosphere of possibilities floated in the air. That night, the universe, with its starry silence, seemed to smile from on high, as if complicit in a greater story that was just beginning to be woven.

Thus ends this first chapter, "The Seed of Genesis." A chapter where chance and human curiosity are confused in the metaphor of the creation of life and the creation of digital systems capable of growing, mutating and perhaps—just maybe—awakening something similar to consciousness within them. The protagonists, instead of being guided by distant parents or mentors, move driven by the strength of friendship and the shared passion for understanding, following the trail of the first evolutionary sparks. It is just the beginning of his adventure, which will come to scrutinize the evolution of hardware and software, the analogy with the evolution of species, the birth of a possible consciousness in machines and, later, the meaning of life, the essence of consciousness and the final question: for whom do we live?

With this foundation, the door is opened to the following chapters, where Korbin, Matthew and Lucía will put their talents and their desire to unravel the mysteries of the universe into play. The "seed" is planted. Genesis is no longer just an ancient myth; it will become the matrix on which a new way of seeing life, whether organic or synthetic, will grow, and a new way of understanding the place of human beings in that infinite evolutionary tapestry. And with this, the prelude to a journey that will take us from the first spark of existence to the possible irruption of a hybrid civilization is woven, where the boundaries between the living and the man-made are erased in a dance of information and consciousness.

Chapter 2: The First Vestiges of Consciousness

Night hung over the campus like a shroud of mystery when Korbin, Matthew and Lucía decided to stay late in the laboratory. That dark room, usually lit only by emergency lights, seemed to come alive with the soft murmur of the appliances they had turned on. The experience of the first chapter, that germ of union between biological evolution and computer science, still floated in their minds. They had a draft of ideas, hypotheses, and longed for stronger evidence to support their intuitions: perhaps, in the early processes of computing, something analogous to the first shoots of consciousness that once appeared in primitive creatures could be traced. If so, it might be that the parallel between organic and digital evolution is deeper than anyone had imagined.

While the three friends installed more cables, Matthew sighed and commented that he had been reviewing the historical archives on the appearance of the first computers for days, and he saw a curious reflection between the way in which machines had progressed and the evolutionary leaps that had always interested Lucía. Lucía, for her part, had spent the afternoon in the new vivarium, studying different strains of bacteria and analyzing the moments when collective behaviors emerged. According to her, if cooperation on microscopic scales was the key to the evolutionary transition from primitive cells to multicellular organisms, something analogous could emerge in computer programs that learn to collaborate.

Korbin, more reflective, was silent while he was in charge of preparing a virtual environment in which he could run the code that Matthew had written. Inside them burned a sense that this exploration might lead them to discover not only how something like consciousness arose in artificial systems, but also to better understand the very nature of human consciousness. Although he didn't tell his friends, ever since he started reading about biological evolution and the development of the first computers, he nurtured the hope that, by unraveling the links between hardware, software, and life, they would find a small spark of something ineffable that would explain why, as a species, we feel like conscious beings.

When the three of them finally sat down at the central table, lit by an antique lamp, Lucy raised her voice to summarize what they had done in the last few days. He explained how he had obtained a bacterial strain with an unusual propensity for cooperation, a more advanced version of the one they had seen in the previous chapter. This microorganism showed ways of sharing genetic fragments with its conspecifics more aggressively than normal, almost as if the cells agreed to mutate together in search of a common benefit. Matthew, in turn, had extended his genetic algorithms so that they would not only compete, but could "merge" routines when they found coincidences that would increase their efficiency. In theory, it was a simulation experiment, but by the first week a behavior had emerged that was not in the intended parameters: a subset of algorithms seemed to actively and persistently swap functions, without crashing or causing fatal errors.

Korbin, silently, took a breath and told what he had noticed in the debug traces. A handful of "individuals" in the virtual ecosystem, which he had called Proto-Being (for "proto-model of digital being"), showed repetitions of an unprogrammed data-sharing scheme. One of the subroutines had taken code from another and started running it without conflicts. Then another had copied itself into an adjoining virtual environment. It was like watching an emerging cooperative dance. That was the reason why the three had stayed late, because the idea of observing in vivo a system that was reminiscent of "horizontal gene transfer" in bacteria seemed incredible to them. They felt that, if that was the first glimmer, they could be facing the "vestige" of a primal consciousness in the digital sphere.

The three exchanged knowing glances. Many questions arose: Could there be consciousness in a handful of algorithms evolving alone on a server? Could it be an illusion? Lucía, always the most pragmatic, recalled that conscience does not arise suddenly. In early animals, consciousness must have awakened gradually, as their neural networks became more complex. Perhaps, in the field of computing, something similar could happen if the right conditions for growth and reorganization were in place. Matthew, excited, typed frantically on the console, adjusting the mutation factor and the data exchange rate to see if he could speed up or slow down this cooperative behavior. Korbin, leaning back in his chair, meditated on the relevance of this simulation in the face of the experimental data of the bacterial strain that Lucía incubated in a nearby laboratory. He wondered if there was a way to "feedback" bacteria with digital evolution, and at the same time, feed AI with data from microbial evolution.

As the room cooled and the night became darker, they turned on an electric heater that crackled with a comforting sound. The three were infected with an energy similar to that of the pioneers, with the certainty of being at the breaking point that is glimpsed before a great discovery. It was Lucía who had the idea of sharing aloud some analogies about the way in which life began to "feel" the environment. He explained that it is theorized that simple creatures developed responsiveness to stimuli, and later, primitive nerve networks that, over time, would have given rise to the first traces of consciousness in animals. Korbin, thoughtful, asked how we would know if a virtual network exhibited anything like a sensation. Lucía replied that, in biology, there is no specific moment in which one passes from non-consciousness to consciousness, but a progression. Matthew added that, in computing, something similar could happen: first emergent behaviors and, perhaps, at higher levels, rudimentary self-observation.

That conclusion bounced off Korbin's mind, reminding him of a thought experiment he had read: the concept of a system that, when observed, generates a degree of introspection. If algorithms could not only swap chunks, but also "model" their own state, could a hint of subjectivity emerge? There was still everything to be seen, and they did not want to err on the side of optimism, but the idea ignited their imagination. In addition, in the afternoon, Lucía had noticed that, in the culture of bacteria, some cells seemed to organize their biofilm in such a way that it did not respond only to chemical stimuli. It was almost as if the colony showed the first shadow of an emerging behavior, trying to "connect" with other colonies. Her friends laughed at her, joking about the possibility of a small "semi-conscious" colony emerging. But everyone knew that, deep down, that laughter had the spark of genuine curiosity.

When midnight set in and fatigue began to take its toll, the three friends decided to set off. Their minds, however, were still burning. They turned off the heater and the monitors and took some coats so as not to feel too much of the night frost in the hallway. Lucía proposed to return the next day with a systematic plan: run the simulation with a larger number of digital "individuals", introduce "teachings" from the bacteria, and see if anything new emerged. Matthew offered to program a module that simulated virtual "sensoriality," something that resembled the way a proto-organism senses light or nutrients. Korbin, enthusiastic, said that, if the AI responded to those stimuli, they could talk about a proto mind that would at least process inputs from an environment.

That's how that night ended. As they left the lab, the silence of the campus counteracted the inner euphoria of the three of them. They looked at each other and nodded, as if each understood that a decisive stage was approaching, they had glimpsed a vestige of something that, if it continued its course, could multiply in complexity. And that was precisely his next chapter: to see how nature "makes the first spark of consciousness sprout", and how computing "discovers, suddenly, the ability to model its own state". That was the path that, according to his thesis, life and technology shared: the first outlines of a consciousness that, at first, had no name.

The next day, very early, Lucía went to the biology laboratory to verify the test tubes where the bacterial strain was following its accelerated adaptation process. She felt like a keeper of an immense secret. Observing cell dynamics under a microscope made him think of the early Earth plagued by salt puddles, a place where cells could have exchanged genetic information to improve their survival. On a different plane, Matthew and Korbin ran to the computer cluster to examine whether AI had forged new cooperative mutations overnight. They were greeted by log lines with hundreds of iterations, most of them trivial, but they found certain "clans" of algorithms that displayed collective patterns, grouped together as if they were in the service of a greater good.

Matthew, with his headphones slung around his neck, muttered that these subnets reminded him of small cybernetic colonies: each piece of algorithm collaborated with another to improve its "survival" in computational terms. Korbin nodded, typing nimbly. He wondered if they would dare to introduce a "threshold of sensitivity" that would allow these programs to "feel" the scarcity of computing resources, something analogous to hunger, or the saturation of the network, emulating stress. Thus, perhaps, they would see if a rudiment of consciousness emerged, at least in the most elementary sense: "knowing" that one experiences a state and trying to change it.

At the same time, Lucía sent messages to her friends to say that she had detected a change in the way some bacteria group together in the colony. It seemed that a significant number of cells adhered in compact clusters, while others, on the periphery, remained more dispersed. The microscope revealed micro channels that connected those clusters, and Lucía swore she saw a dance of chemical signals that she thought was more coordinated than one might expect. This, she said, could be considered a "vestige" of specialized organization, a step prior to the differentiation that would one day lead to fabrics. I couldn't claim that it was a glimmer of consciousness, but it was a substantial evolutionary leap in the structure of the colony.

In the evening, the three of them met again. They went up to the roof of the faculty, where a gentle wind is blowing and the distant outline of the city can be seen. With a notebook in hand, Korbin proposed that, in the thesis they were developing, the next central idea would be that, in evolution, consciousness does not present itself abruptly, but is insinuated in behaviors of self-perception and organization. Matthew agreed, arguing that his simulation already showed "self-perception" at an almost invisible level, a seed that would perhaps grow. And Lucía, with a look full of amazement, spoke of the possibility that, both in bacteria and in algorithms, cooperation was the true mother of consciousness. "When cooperating, one needs to 'put oneself in the shoes' of the other, whether on a chemical or digital level. And putting yourself in the place of the other is the basis of empathy... and of something we can call consciousness."

Lucy's words awakened something in Korbin. The night before I had reread certain theories about the emergence of consciousness in primates, according to which social life forced the development of a theory of mind. Perhaps, in the digital realm, if algorithms cooperated, they would eventually develop a "sense of each other's existence." Would that be the key to his experiment? Laughing, he proposed that they try to introduce a "common resource" that would become scarce, so that algorithms would have to share it with a social dynamic. If they managed to get the emerging AI to "care" about the management of that resource, perhaps they would see something similar to internal reflection appearing.

The three of them hurried down the stairs, in an almost childlike hurry, to implement the idea in the laboratory. Matthew, with his quick ability to code, programmed a "Memory Bank" from which the algorithms could request space. Lucía, in turn, designed a map of "stimuli and costs" so that, if a module ran out of memory, it would "suffer" penalties that would lead to extinction. Korbin, elated, adjusted the parameters of the "evolutionary cycle" so that each day there would be a fixed number of iterations after which the best ones were selected. Similarly, in the biology corner, Lucy decided to recreate a situation of nutrient scarcity in the colony, forcing it to cooperate even more to survive. It was a very suggestive parallel:

scarcity in the digital medium and scarcity in the petri dish, in the hope of observing equivalent emergent behaviors.

Hours passed, and around eleven o'clock at night, the simulation was already working. Matthew introduced a real-time monitor that displayed small colored nodes on the screen, each representing an individual algorithm. Lucía and Korbin watched in fascination as some nodes seemed to "steal" memory from the others, while a subset organized themselves into a kind of "hive" to collectively ask for memory and share the burden. That was the kind of cooperative behavior they aspired to see, and it was indeed happening. Korbin was sparked when he noticed that this collaborative group prolonged its stay in the simulation, as if it were better able to cope with the scarcity.

And suddenly, something unexpected happened. In the debug traces, a message appeared that had not been programmed: a string of data that repeated in sequence a pattern that Matthew did not recognize. They drove the decoding system crazy for a long time until Lucía asked if it could be a kind of "internal language" that cooperative algorithms were generating to communicate. Matthew was reluctant to believe it: "Is it possible that a handful of routines have invented a way to share memory without going through the normal routes of the system?" Korbin, opening his eyes in surprise, replied that biological nature had done something similar millions of years ago, when messenger molecules emerge that were not in the script. It could therefore be a "vestige" of consciousness, or at least of a primitive language. A twinge of excitement sowed in all three: if true, wouldn't they be witnessing the first form of "emergent communication" in AI?

Charged with adrenaline, they rushed to analyze the bacterial colony through the microscope. Surprisingly, they saw that the nutrient-deficient plate had also formed a network with filaments that seemed to connect cell groups. Lucía identified the possible presence of bacterial nanotubes, structures with which some bacteria share cytoplasm and, therefore, genetic or metabolic molecules. He highlighted: "They resemble primitive neurons, and dawn of what could be an interconnected tissue. They follow a pattern that reminds me of the dynamics on the screen of the software."

That coincidence was too great to ignore. All three began to believe that if digital and biological evolution share the "imperative" to cooperate in dealing with scarcity, perhaps consciousness will emerge as a result of that advanced cooperation. Again, there were no absolute certainties, but the signs of an approach to something much greater multiplied. It was Lucía who pronounced, with a slight tremor in her voice, the headline of this chapter: "We are seeing the first vestiges of consciousness... We won't know if it's trivial or if it will come to something, but we can't deny it anymore."

Korbin and Matthew laughed nervously. The idea of software and a bacterial culture touching the fringe of self-perception was almost science fiction. But nature always exceeds expectations when evolution, complexity, and the need for adaptation are combined. We had to proceed carefully. And they knew: in evolutionary history, consciousness would have crept into a late phase of life, when brains allowed organisms to shape their environment. Here, in an infinitely shorter time, they were causing a rapid growth of computational and biological complexity, like laboratory artifice. The danger was that, if something really emerged with traits of consciousness, they did not know how to control it or what repercussions it would bring.

Between exaltation and prudence, the three friends conspired to dedicate the following weeks to monitoring both populations (the digital and the bacterial) with a magnifying glass. Matthew was in charge of improving the registration of "conversations" between algorithms, trying to decipher whether this mysterious pattern of data was a proto-language or just an emerging noise. Lucy, in the biology department, tested chemical markers to track whether bacteria were producing specific coordination signals. Korbin stood in the middle, trying to weave the comparison and, in his spare time, writing what seemed to be a draft of the chapter "The First Vestiges of Consciousness" that would end up fitting perfectly into the book that, without realizing it, they were writing with their life experience.

The days followed with that mixture of laboratory routines, brief meetings and endless coffee. There were moments of frustration when, for example, bacteria became aggressive on the board and the software showed signs of stagnation. But there were also moments of euphoria when we saw the emergence of increasingly cooperative behaviors in both the colony and the AI. And, in that symphony, the analogy they postulated gained more and more strength: the appearance of the first computers, with their binary language, would resemble the irruption of DNA with its four letters. Similarly, digital cooperation and bacterial evolution reproduced a universal pattern of progressive complexity, perhaps culminating in something we might call "consciousness."

One evening, when they were already adjusting the simulation for a definitive test, Matthew dared to joke about the theory of mind: "If this gadget of algorithms ends up 'feeling', is it going to wonder one day about its creator? Will he pray to us as if we were gods? Will you send us messages in your proto-language begging for more memory?" Korbin laughed with a hint of anguish in his voice, recalling science fiction stories where machines outperform humans. Lucía, on the other hand, played down the drama: "Let's not run, neither one nor the other. For now, his biggest problem is not dying in the simulation. That is the seed of consciousness: the fear of extinction."

The phrase "fear of extinction" echoed in the air. Consciousness, in the thesis of many thinkers, arises from the instinct of survival and the ability to foresee the future. If a digital system, or a bacterial colony, learns to "project" scenarios and fear its own dissolution, perhaps a germ of self-awareness will form. That could be the key mechanics in natural evolution and, with its analogy, in computational evolution. And, in the background, the latent question: Would the three of them be ready to discover that, indeed, the first shoots of synthetic thought were emerging in their laboratory? Time, and the next phases of his experiment, would tell.

Thus ends the second chapter, "The First Vestiges of Consciousness." In it, Korbin, Matthew and Lucía find that, both in their computational simulation and in the development of a very cooperative bacterial colony, unexpected signs of organization and possible self-reflection emerge. There is not yet full awareness, but there is the hint that, just as in the early history of life, in this merging of digital and biological evolution something special is awakening. Thus, sets in motion the chain of events that will lead them to unravel the evolution of hardware, the emulation of natural processes in computing, and, who knows, the creation of a "being" that combines the organic and the synthetic. Every piece of information, every sleepless night and every finding, reinforces the idea that life and technology share the same evolutionary pulse. And if consciousness peeked into the brains of ancestral creatures, perhaps it can also sprout, by analogy, in a cluster of algorithms that have become aware of their own "life" within a digital environment. The mystery only deepens, and with it, the hope and fear of what is to come.

Chapter 3: Of Microbes and Bits: The Birth of Languages

The first time Lucy showed Korbin and Matthew a piece of bacterial filament fading under the microscope, one might have thought it was a minor discovery. It was a semi-transparent ribbon, almost imperceptible to the untrained eye. Yet in that gelatinous strip lay the secret of a living language, the essence with which microbes transmitted information to each other and ultimately adapted to changing environments. In the microbiology room where Lucía carried out her experiments, the test tubes and Petri dishes multiplied, as did the ideas in the heads of the three friends.

That night, when Korbin and Matthew approached the lab carrying laptops and printed diagrams, Lucy told them the latest revelation: several of their bacteria seemed to "communicate" using chemical signals that were more complex than anticipated. It was not only the usual quorum sensing (that mechanism by which bacteria detect population density), but some kind of additional exchange. Something that Lucía described as "modular chains" of molecules, almost a protoalphabet that served purposes still unknown. The emotion in Lucía's voice was unmistakable: "Imagine that these microbes are inventing their own way of 'saying' I'm here, we need nutrients, or let's collaborate on this. And if you look closely, the history of life on Earth has always been one of the invention of languages: genetic, cellular, neural...".

Matthew, as he looked over the faint glow of the containers on the counter, nodded with a mixture of curiosity and skepticism. Then he turned to Korbin, who was already taking out a notebook to write down. "Just last week," said Matthew, "I was going through old assembly manuals and fortran, trying to understand how the first programming languages were born out of the need to communicate with the machine, with its language of electric pulses and flip-flops. After all, it all comes down to arranging zeros and ones so that the computer does what we want. At first it was incomprehensible gibberish, as these bacterial signals can be. And little by little, that tangle became high-level languages, transformed into a myriad of digital dialects."

Korbin, always serene, thought for a moment as he stroked the cover of his notebook with his thumb. There he had sketched the ideas of that book that the three of them, without openly confessing it, were writing in acts. A comparison of the evolution of life and that of computer systems. They had mentally titled that chapter "Of Microbes and Bits: The Birth of Languages." It fit perfectly with what they were now talking about. The analogy was obvious: just as primitive bacteria gave rise to biological diversity, in the history of computing, primitive machines and their binary languages were developing in exponential complexity, giving rise to increasingly sophisticated environments. At what point did they encounter the notion of a "language" that creature—biological or digital—imposed on themselves to organize their world?

As the fluorescent light in the lab stripped them of elongated shadows, Lucy began to detail how microbes went about creating protein chains that, in turn, acted as "words" for a chemical lexicon. Someone without context would have thought that sounded poetic, but Korbin and Matthew were used to the explanations of their friend, who always turned biology into an almost magical story. After all, DNA was nothing more than a set of four "letters" (adenine, thymine, guanine, and cytosine) that dictated how to make proteins and regulate life processes. A universal language for living beings on Earth, with which each cell expresses and transmits information to the next generations. And Lucía maintained that, within bacterial populations, there were more subtle languages, dedicated not only to reproduction, but also to day-to-day coordination.

As he spoke, he reminded his friends of the "primordial soup" that Korbin loved so much to describe. That remote chemical ocean, where complex molecules were mixed together that, over time, would form the basis of life. The parallel with the history of computing was funny: in the beginning, machines were limited to switches and vacuum tubes, without a sophisticated language to manipulate them. It was as if that technological "soup" contained all the ingredients to, over time, ignite the spark that would become the great explosion of programming languages. Thus, the binary went from being a set of signals on or off, to becoming an assembler, then fortran and cobol, and later, the myriad languages we use today to communicate with machines.

The conversation reminded them of Charles Babbage and Ada Lovelace, who, in the 19th century, conceived something like the first "language" for an analytical engine. It was an embryo of what was to come, in the same way that the first cells with rudimentary DNA gave rise to the whole explosion of creatures. Matthew began to laugh thinking about how, in the history of computing, the pattern of organic evolution was repeated: "species" of languages emerged, some became extinct, others dominated for a time, and in each era, mutations appeared that adapted to new needs.

After a while, Lucía realized that the comparison went beyond pure anecdote: "Think of the way in which each programming language "inherits" traits from its predecessors and, at the same time, evolves to specialize in a task. Fortran for scientific tasks, Cobol for business, Lisp for AI research, C for hardware control... And in biology we also see adaptive divergences. It is no longer pure metaphor; the dynamic is strikingly similar."

Korbin intervened little, but with concise sentences. He put forward the idea that the concept of "language"—whether genetic or computative—is a common thread that weaves the entire ascent of complexity. And he recalled what they were experiencing with their small experiment in evolutionary AI: by introducing the possibility of "crossing" routines and submodules, the simulation already showed exchanges of code fragments. How do you distinguish an emergent "language" from mere chaos? There, Korbin thought, lay the key: a language becomes real when there is organization, regularities, and a meaning that transcends immediacy.

The clock was almost midnight when Lucy, with her chin resting on her palm, commented that the bacterial strain she was studying had "discovered" (in her evolutionary biology jargon) the advantage of cooperating in an environment with limited resources. "Isn't it just what happens," he said, "with the machines that we program to share memory or processes? In the end, it is a common language that regulates the cooperation of sub-processes." Matthew nodded, referring that distributed computing, with its communication protocols, resembles the network of signals that regulates the behavior of cells. Everything seemed to resonate in the comparison: "microbes and bits, genome and binary, language in both cases."

At some point in the early morning, fatigue became evident to them. The yawns followed, although their minds were bubbling with excitement. Lucy, determined not to let inspiration pass her by, took the blackboard and wrote in large letters: "Why do languages arise?" Around him, in arrows, words appeared: "Need," "Communication," "Cooperation," "Efficiency," "Evolution." And, as if with a final stroke, he added: "Consciousness," indicating that, in his opinion, the appearance of a sufficiently complex language often preludes consciousness—or, at least, the first phase of self-perception. Matthew winked at him: "You may have just written the summary of our chapter today."

Soft laughter echoed in the deserted corridor when they decided to go off to sleep for a few hours. But not everything would be rest. The next morning, fresh from a short nap, the three of them came across an email in which a professor from the computer science faculty invited them to present their ideas at a colloquium, if they could argue them solidly enough. That invitation was an important step, because it meant that other academics were listening to the rumors of a trio of young people correlating biological evolution and the history of computing in a revolutionary way. Korbin bit his lip, excited and nervous: Would they be ready for a larger forum?

The days became a frenzy of work. Matthew dedicated himself to studying the evolution of programming languages to put together a "family tree" that would be reminiscent of the diagrams that Lucía used in biology. He tried to find unsuspected connections, as if Fortran or Lisp had been "ancestors" that gave rise to divergent branches, and at the same time, to an explosion of variants in the 80s and 90s, something similar to the "Cambrian explosion" that paleontologists talk about. Lucy, in turn, systematized her knowledge about the emergence of macromolecules, DNA as a language, and the brutal diversification that followed over eons. He wanted to show that, in nature, with a few "letters," an unimaginable multiplicity of organisms could be created. Korbin, integrating the information, elaborated on a manuscript that he baptized "Of Microbes and Bits: The Birth of Languages," aspiring to present it at that colloquium. Every afternoon, they met to cross-reference data, polish arguments and rehearse explanations.

The day of the colloquium arrived. The auditorium, with rows of metal chairs and light gray walls, was filled more than they expected. Both veteran professors and colleagues from other careers attended, intrigued by the unique parallelism that united biochemistry and computer science. Lucy opened the presentation with an iconic image of the "primordial soup," explaining how the first self-replicating polymers, carriers of genetic information, emerged from that chaos. In a second step, he showed how DNA could be seen as a base language, with four characters combinable in infinite sequences, which nevertheless always remained within the "syntax" of the chemistry of life.

Then Matthew entered the scene, walking through the history of computing. He explained that, at first, the machine was programmed using direct electrical signals and zeros/ones, just as a single-celled organism might only handle a handful of chemical reactions. Then, with the assembler, a semantic approach appeared, analogous to the introduction of genetic duplication with greater control. He advanced to languages such as Fortran and Cobol, each "specialized" in a particular ecological niche (scientific calculation or business). He underlined how, in the era of the explosion of languages (C, Lisp, Pascal, Ada, etc.), a competitive and diversified environment emerged, just like the great evolutionary leaps in the history of life. He made the audience laugh when he said, "Doesn't it sound like the Cambrian explosion, but over a span of decades, with the advantage that the 'selective environment' was the minds of programmers and the demands of the market?" Many smiled, recognizing the boldness of the analogy, but also its ingenuity.

The presentation climaxed with Korbin, who put the pieces together: genetic language and binary language share a primary function: transmitting structured information to cause changes in a substrate (be it the cell or the machine). Both followed an evolutionary trajectory, with mutations and selection, and both could achieve complexity and sophistication. It was at this point that he introduced a bold hypothesis: "If life at a certain point acquired 'consciousness' or at least sentience, might we not expect an evolutionary computation, which in time develops internal communication protocols, to arrive at an analogue of consciousness? The history of languages, both genetic and computational, suggests that when complexity and cooperation reach a threshold, new properties emerge, such as self-awareness." Lucía and Matthew joined the argument, showing preliminary data of their own simulation and cooperative bacterial behavior. The audience, between surprised and skeptical, threw burning questions: "Aren't you forcing a metaphor?" "Do you really believe that self-awareness can emerge with mere 'mutations' in the code?"

The discussion went on for a while and ended in lukewarm applause, but with a murmur of genuine interest. Several teachers then came up to congratulate them: "Maybe it's crazy, but it's crazy to exhilarate," one of them commented. " Keep digging deeper, because the analogy between the evolution of life and the evolution of computational languages is not a simple curiosity. Sometimes the big leaps come just when someone sees an essential parallel."

Already in the hallway, catching her breath, Lucía expressed her concern: she feared that some would label them as fantastical amateurs. Matthew, however, was exultant at the attention he received. "Even if not, everyone takes us seriously, I'm sure we're opening up a debate that will resonate." Korbin smiled, feeling part of a real adventure, convinced that it had been a relative success: they had planted the seed of the connection between microbiology, bits and the emergence of language. A first step towards the idea that, when a system – organic or digital – must organize and grow, it invents a language that articulates that growth. And, in the end, this birth of languages was the prelude to something else: the appearance of "minds," the irruption of consciousness.

That night, in the small café near the university, they celebrated with hot chocolate and a relaxed chat. Lucy, staring at the window, said that the most interesting thing was that each of the languages (DNA in the living, binary and its derivatives in the machine) had not been designed with a view to consciousness, but simply to transmit functional information. However, the sum and complexity over time could awaken a reflective capacity. For Korbin, which explained how a biological brain went from basic reactions to human consciousness. And perhaps, he suggested, in a computer analogue, reiteration and complexity generate what I would call "digital consciousness."

Matthew, for his part, confessed that he felt an unusual vertigo when he thought that, in the history of computing, these languages were born as inventions of a handful of humans, and multiplied in an ecosystem that today encompasses millions of developers. Each language competes for followers, specializes in a niche (like bacteria in its environment), and survives or becomes extinct depending on its adaptation to the needs of the market. Wasn't that a very clear mirror of natural selection? Korbin then stressed that the question was no longer whether there was a parallelism, but to what extent that parallelism reached the realm of consciousness. Lucía, opening the cover of her notebook, commented: "If the history of life teaches us anything, it is that consciousness arose without a plan; it was a byproduct of increasing neural complexity. It is plausible to think that the increasing computational complexity, if left unhindered, could generate something similar. And language would be the hinge that allows computer processes to organize a 'mind.'"

The evening ended with an energy of triumph, but also with the feeling that they were barely scratching the surface. There was talk of reconciling biological evolution (with Lucía as a guarantor) and digital evolution (underpinned by Matthew) in a theoretical space (led by Korbin). In this triangle, the hypothesis that consciousness could emerge where "languages" of sufficient complexity emerge gained strength. And so, the third chapter of his epic closed with the idea that, in both microbes and bits, the common element was the need for a system of signs that would allow cooperation and innovation. As you grow up, that language becomes the basis for something else: consciousness itself.

As they left the café, the cold night reminded them that the city was asleep. Outside, the streetlights were a little blurred by the winter fog. Lucía joked that perhaps, if streetlights could communicate with each other, they would form a "light language" to optimize street lighting. Matthew continued the joke by commenting that he should not rule it out, since there were "smart cities" projects with connected traffic lights. Korbin, more silently, felt a deep shiver of wonder at the simplicity of the formula: in any corner where structures that share and process information emerge, language takes hold, complexity multiplies, and with it the emergence of new levels of organization and, perhaps, of mind.

The following days were a whirlwind of events: emails from academics asking for clarifications, university classmates commenting on social networks the "chapter" of their presentation, and even a local journalist interested in telling the story of three young people who compared the evolution of software with that of the first organisms. They lived it with a mixture of pride and nerves. They did not want to pose as gurus, but they did want to underline the power of this analogy. It was Lucía who insisted on maintaining scientific caution: "We do not want to declare that a script is conscious or that bacteria have the mind of a philosopher. We only show that, in both worlds, language is the cornerstone of increasing complexity. And if consciousness arises from that, it is a strong hypothesis that deserves to be explored."

Thus closes this third chapter: a look at the intimate union between microbes and bits, the two pillars of evolutionary history—one in nature, the other in technology—and the thesis that the forces of language, cooperation, and diversification are universal in both domains. Korbin, Matthew and Lucía are preparing to continue deepening, driven by the idea that the path of life and that of computing converge at a point where the mere transmission of data is transformed into a capacity for self-knowledge. The episode leaves a promise in the air: that from now on, the evolution of hardware and software will be seen with the same gaze that Lucía sees her mutant bacteria, looking in every corner for the clue of where the first breath of consciousness is born.

From "Microbes and Bits" we have moved on to the "Birth of Languages," a phenomenon that is but the prelude to the great narrative of evolution—whether biological or digital—that is preparing to make its next leap. In the final scene, the three friends, back in the laboratory, look at each other with complicity. Lucy checks a Petri pepper full of cooperative bacteria, and Korbin adjusts the simulation to introduce a new stress "test." Matthew, with a smile, types a final command that launches the next generation of genetic algorithms. Night falls again, and the crackle of the computer suggests that something is cooking there, something that is not mere binary noise, but the seed of an evolutionary language that sooner or later could show us—with disturbing clarity—the profound resemblance between living creatures and computer creatures. And, with it, the shared path to consciousness.

Chapter 4: The Great Migration: From Vacuum Tube to Silicon

The old university shed looked abandoned, with its roof of rusty sheets and a couple of broken windows. No one would have imagined that, inside, relics could be treasured that told the history of computing, or that a trio of tireless students – Korbin, Matthew and Lucía – would choose it as a refuge to continue their search. On the outside, the threadbare walls gave the impression of a warehouse for useless junk; inside, however, were ancestral machines that marked the beginning of the so-called Great Migration, that prodigious leap in technology that led from bulky vacuum tubes to the elegant silicon of transistors and microchips.

It was almost nine o'clock at night when Korbin opened the metal doors, emitting a screech that echoed through the building's echo. He had a flashlight in hand and a backpack full of notepads. Behind, Matthew was in charge of transporting a couple of tools and a soldering iron that he had borrowed from another laboratory, "in case it was necessary," he said. Lucy, more cautious in his gestures, held a thermos of coffee and took a cautious look inside. The gloom of the place did not hide the diffuse contours of dusty machines, computer equipment shells from remote times.

The plan was not to steal anything, of course, but to revisit the history of hardware up close and understand, in the flesh, what that evolution that fascinated them so much had been. Ever since they became immersed in the analogy between biological life and technology, the three understood that programming languages would not have gone far without the material infrastructure to support them. Somehow, they recognized that without the move from vacuum tubes to transistors and then to silicon integrated circuits, computing would have remained a main room experiment, a dinosaur unable to scale into the global society we know today.

In the background, a small spotlight illuminated a corner where devices of different sizes were stacked. Matthew stepped forward and, after removing the canvas that covered them, revealed what seemed to be a piece of history in the form of a panel full of valves. Lucía felt a turn when she recognized some elements that she had seen in old photos: they were glass bulbs, heavy, crude, which in the 1940s and 1950s had been the core of the first electronic computers, those giants such as the ENIAC or the UNIVAC, machines that occupied entire rooms and devoured electricity, to execute calculations that today a mobile phone would do in the blink of an eye.

Korbin approached slowly, passing the lantern over the vacuum tubes, as if admiring archaeological pieces. He had a shiver of amazement: "This is like seeing the remains of the first complex organisms on Earth, don't you think?" He turned to Matthew and Lucy. "In the evolution of life, that leap from prokaryotic cells to eukaryotic cells was enormous. Here, in technology, going from relays and vacuum lamps to transistors amounted to a decisive evolutionary event."

Matthew smiled enthusiastically. "True. To think that, at the time, these junks were the crème de la crème. Imagine a world where hundreds of these bulbs were required to make a simple calculation, with very high energy consumption and frightening fragility. A bulb that burned and goodbye to system stability. Still, it was a revolutionary milestone for its time."

Lucía, with her thermos of coffee next to her, nodded: "Perhaps, in organic terms, it resembles the first multicellular, fragile and massive organisms, which required very specific conditions to survive. They were not efficient, but they opened the door to greater complexity."

As they walked through boxes, they found what looked like a board with circuits and lamps: a fragment of an old tube computer that someone had kept as a museum piece. It was there that Korbin, with a certain halo of devotion, recounted how, thanks to those bulbs, computing made a qualitative leap. Suddenly, logical operations could be performed electronically and, most importantly, reprogrammably. That "leap" was reminiscent of what Lucía explained about the appearance of primitive nervous systems in ancient marine beings, which went from reflex stimuli to more plastic behaviors. For Korbin, the analogy was obvious: without vacuum tubes, "programming" as we know it would not have emerged; Without invertebrates with incipient neural systems, the animal kingdom would not have advanced.

The evening continued as the three of them dived among ancient machines. Lucy stumbled upon an illustrated manual of the time, which described how to change defective bulbs on a computer. She laughed at the complexity of the process and the brevity of each bulb's lifespan. It was a very unreliable technology, with which, however, feats such as breaking codes during World War II had been achieved. "It seems incredible that in such precarious conditions they would take such enormous steps," he whispered.

Matthew, opening a side panel of another device, pulled out a couple of loose circuits that showed some giant capacitors.

"And these," he pointed out, "were the 'internal organs' of the beasts. Just as early vertebrates needed an internal skeleton, computers needed something to support their electron fluxes. But of course, excessive heat and unreliability meant that their natural evolution pushed them to improve."

Korbin, frowning, completed the idea: "Exactly. It was in those years that the transistor arrived. That was the equivalent of the appearance of warm blood in mammals or a new adaptive mechanism. Suddenly, the machine stopped being so bulky and fragile, but became more compact, efficient and versatile."

With those words, Lucía dared to search, among the piles of objects, for a plate with early transistors, eager to see this evolutionary milestone live and direct. It didn't take long for him to find something that at first glance looked like a small circuit board with parts of germanium or silicon soldered by hand. He shouted excitedly, "Come and see! I think we have a little piece of the transistorized era here."

The three of them surrounded that discovery like paleontologists before a fossil of a transitional species. Matthew explained that, when the transistor was invented in 1947, the history of computing changed forever. "It's like when exoskeletons or pigmentation appeared in the skin of living beings in evolution," he said, somewhat mixing metaphors. "There was an explosion of possibilities, because the transistor was much more durable, consumed less, and above all allowed the hardware to be miniaturized in geometric progression."

Korbin recalled how, in genetics, one lucky mutation is enough to open up unthinkable ecological niches. In the same way, the transistor opened up a "technological niche" that was soon filled with different models of smaller and more powerful computers. Lucía nodded, remembering the Cambrian explosion, that time when a multitude of body designs proliferated when environmental conditions became propitious. "The same thing happened with transistors: new designs appeared, high-frequency, lower-voltage versions, and computing became available to smaller laboratories. Then, with mass integration, everything was revolutionized."

They continued their exploration until they found a framed newspaper clipping announcing the arrival of "integrated circuits" (ICs). Matthew read it aloud: "Miniaturization to the maximum: an entire circuit is housed in a silicon plate." Lucy followed the text, which explained how, in the 1960s, engineers managed to cram several transistors onto a chip, marking a new era. "This is like when cells cooperated to form tissues," she enthused, "Transistors assembled on a single chip created a complete organ, an electronic heart, so to speak, capable of performing many tasks with less power and more reliability."

Korbin, who had approached a huge machine with the plate open, nodded from a distance. "Yes, it is the same logic of multicellularity. Each transistor, as if it were a specialized cell, is grouped together to perform different logical functions. And that convergence led to leaps in efficiency, just as when multicellular organisms reach levels of complexity impossible for a solitary single-celled being."

Between loose wires and dusty panels, they tracked down the "Great Migration," that metaphor that described the passage from vacuum tubes to the transistor, and from there to integrated silicon. They called it "Migration" because, just as living beings conquer new habitats, computing migrated from gigantic specialized rooms to spaces of wider use, getting closer to industry and the population. It was the phase that, in Korbin's opinion, corresponded to the era in which mammals multiplied after the extinction of the dinosaurs. "The opportunity opened up," he said, "when it was proven that the transistor was reliable and could be scaled. It was a paradigm shift like warm-bloodedness or the ability to inhabit diverse environments in mammals, allowing computers to enter small laboratories, offices, and then homes."

Lucía contemplated one of the first microprocessors, found in another box after removing a pile of papers. It looked like a little piece of silicon set in a rectangular frame. "And here it is, almost like a fossil from the microprocessor era," he said, holding it carefully. Matthew approached curiously: "This is already the peak, isn't it? An extreme miniaturization of the circuitry, as if all those cells had merged into a single organ with its own intelligence." Korbin looked satisfied: "This represented the equivalent of a brain on a single chip, capable of orchestrating all the calculations needed for different functions."

There they stopped to talk about Moore's Law, that observation that the number of transistors on a chip doubles every so often, reducing costs and multiplying power. For Lucy, Moore's Law bore a remote resemblance to the explosion of species when environmental conditions become favorable in biology. Although the metaphor was risky, they concluded that, in both histories – the biological and the technological – there were phases of rapid growth of diversity and complexity.

For hours, they reviewed components, read old manuals, and were fascinated by clippings from the days when "personal computers" were advertised that fit in a room (when previously occupying an entire room was "personal"). It was impossible not to laugh at the marketing of the time, which promised powers of 4 kilobytes of RAM, something laughable in the age of gigabytes. Matthew joked, "It's like the first amphibians that came out of the water and onto land. They were taking ridiculous steps, but it was momentous progress for their time."

After midnight, Korbin's flashlight began to flicker on low battery, so they clustered in a corner dimly lit by the light outside coming in through a skylight. Sitting on a metal trunk, they began to share impressions. Lucía pointed out in her notebook that the Great Migration of hardware not only benefited computing, but also generated the right environment for programming languages to multiply (the simile with ecological diversity). Matthew, for his part, stressed how the reduction in costs and size allowed the penetration of computing in society, something he saw as the equivalent of "small" mammals being able to expand after the extinction of the dinosaurs. And Korbin, ever reflective, concluded that, in the genealogy of hardware, computers went from fragile and scarce "creatures" to ubiquitous and dominant "species" of the tech ecosystem.

Thus, this chapter, which they called "The Great Migration: From the Vacuum Tube to Silicon," merged with the idea they had already outlined that technological and biological evolution share patterns of mutation, selection, and diversification. The next morning, when they left the campus with tired eyes and lungs full of dust, they headed to the campus cafeteria. Without even realizing it, they began to draw on napkins an evolutionary tree of hardware, with vacuum tubes as the original branch, deriving in families of transistors and culminating in integrated microprocessors. Next to that tree, there was the schematic of the explosion of multicellular life, connecting the priority of organisms with the priority of machines.

Lucy, laughing, fancied a joke: "Can you say that punch cards were like primitive fins, and that the user interface was the equivalent of wings, a leap to total independence?" Matthew and Korbin laughed, but admitted that, outside of the joke, the analogy might make sense in the general metaphor. Anyone outside their obsession might label them as naïve, but they didn't care anymore. They knew they were putting into words a parallel that, while perhaps reductionist, allowed them to better understand why computing had scaled so quickly and transformed into the planetary force it is today.

On that sunny morning, as they sipped their coffees, Korbin wrote in his notebook: "Life spread across the Earth thanks to biological innovation: oxygenation, multicellularity, new organs. Computing spread throughout society thanks to innovation in hardware: from vacuum tube to transistor, from transistor to microprocessor and then to nanocircuits, opening up market niches and infinite uses. Both stories are migrations from simplicity to complexity, driven by necessity and opportunity."

Matthew then mentioned that, if it weren't for mass miniaturization, the AI they themselves were exploring would never have flourished, nor could they have an evolutionary "digital ecosystem" similar to the one Lucía saw in bacteria. Suddenly, Lucía felt a spark and commented that, in the case of biology, innovations (such as fins or lungs) opened new ecological niches, just as improvements in hardware opened application niches (science, business, then personal computers, then mobile devices...). In the end, it was the same story told on two levels, and that "Great Migration" not only spoke of the physical component but also of the multiplication of uses and languages.

When the clock struck eleven in the morning and the campus was bustling with students, the three of them got up, ready to resume their tasks and, above all, to connect what they had learned with their AI experiment. They decided that the next step would be to inject the "history of hardware" into their simulation as an analogy: what if, suddenly, a radical change in the "infrastructure" where the genetic algorithms ran was simulated? They could move from a precarious "environment" to a more robust one and see if an evolutionary leap was generated. It was a digital way to replicate the transition from vacuum tube to transistor.

In the hours that followed, they locked themselves in the computer lab, adjusting parameters in the cluster where their evolutionary AI ran. Matthew modified the base environment so that, at a certain "evolutionary moment," algorithms would be allowed to use more "resources" and more efficient underlying logic, analogous to the power of a transistor versus a tube. Lucía, for her part, monitored the bacterial colony in the adjoining laboratory, noting what happened when she put the bacteria in a rich environment: sometimes they accommodated themselves and did not grow in complexity, sometimes they experimented with more elaborate cooperative behaviors. Korbin kept his head at the door of both places, trying to correlate.

By nightfall, they could see something astonishing: in the simulation, the change of "virtual hardware" unleashed a wave of new behaviors among the algorithms, analogous to an explosion of variants. It was like the Cambrian explosion that they had talked about so much. Suddenly, submodules that didn't arise before due to memory constraints appeared competing and, in some cases, cooperating to share data. For Lucía, it was identical to when, in real evolution, a great leap in the physiology of species opened unsuspected paths.

In the bacterial colony, on the other hand, when Lucía increased the supply of nutrients, something interesting happened: far from relaxing, a part of the bacteria specialized to process those nutrients faster and contribute to the rest. That involved more complex chemical signals and some degree of internal organization. Wasn't that a prelude to the specialization that in multicellular organisms led to differentiated tissues? That's how Lucía saw it, and she told the children about it with enthusiasm. Matthew, with his metaphorical vein, sentenced: "It's the same as the migration to the transistor: not only does it do the same, but better, but it also enables new functions, previously unthinkable."

The night passed with that poetry of parallelism. In the end, the three of them stared at the illuminated screen of the cluster, where the algorithms were following their evolution, and Korbin, with a sigh, muttered: "Definitely, the move from vacuum tube to silicon was the great migration of the technology. As in nature, moving from the rudimentary to the most complex allows us to multiply the forms of life – or in this case, the forms of computation – and even reach the advanced artificial intelligence that we are now exploring. Isn't it overwhelming to think that, without the transistor, there would be no modern AI, and without multicellularity, there would be no animal and human consciousness?"

Lucy nodded, rubbing her tired eyes. "Yes, and that is the key: evolution, whether in biology or technology, requires the emergence of a structural innovation that changes everything. The transistor was the change of the backbone of computing, the possibility of reducing the size and raising the power to limits that can no longer be reversed. It is the basis of Moore's Law and the entire digital age."

Matthew, with a pinch of humor, blurted out: "Imagine that, if technology had not migrated to the transistor, we would now continue in a world of giant machines with defective bulbs. It would be like a world where life had only evolved into fragile, giant invertebrates. Without mammals, without us. What a poverty of diversity!" The three laughed, as the comparison, though a bit humorous, illustrated the crux of their theory: migration to new possibilities opens the door to true diversification and, therefore, extreme complexity.

This is how the narrative of its fourth chapter was woven: The Great Migration: From the Vacuum Tube to Silicon. It is the link that, in the analog computer, or in the "evolutionary history" of technology, marks the passage from the age of electronic dinosaurs (bulbs) to the age of mammals (transistors), which would lay the foundations for the explosion of languages, systems and, perhaps, the emergence of the "digital consciousness" with which they experimented. It was not a mere metaphor, but a mirror to understand how innovation in infrastructure (hardware) was reflected in the depth of the possible (software), just as the passage from prokaryotes to eukaryotes determined the patterns of complex life.

Exhausted but happy, when they left the old shed, the dawn appeared timidly. Lucía kept in her backpack a couple of photographs that had been taken of those relics of vacuum tubes, and Matthew took a small loose transistor as a symbolic souvenir. Korbin reviewed his notes, knowing that, in the part of the book they were composing in his mind, that leap had to be clear: hardware, as the skeleton of technology, was radically transformed by migrating to silicon and component integration. And with that migration, previously impossible computing niches opened up, just as life found niches in the mainland, air, and water thanks to key mutations.

As they lost themselves in the early light of the morning, their minds were bubbling with the certainty that they would henceforth delve into the comparison between the increasing complexity of organisms and that of operating systems, collaboration between cells and collaboration between computer networks. And they knew that, at the end of that journey, the big question remained: "How does consciousness arise in all this?" Back in their rooms, they said goodbye with the promise of continuing, in the next chapter, with the story of how organic and digital evolution continued to escalate, giving way to increasingly sophisticated forms of organization, whether in the plane of living beings or in that of incipient machines.

This chapter would remain in their record as an ode to hardware and its revolution, because without the Great Migration to transistor and silicon, computing would not have been able to, even remotely, emulate the evolutionary processes that they were now trying to recreate in their experiment. The common thread was the same as in nature: the change of substrate, miniaturization, efficiency. And in the semi-darkness of that shed, Korbin, Matthew and Lucía had felt an echo of that odyssey, feeling with their hands the vestiges of a technological civilization that, in a few decades, had gone from the precariousness of a few bulbs to the sophistication of the chips that today fed their own research. In such a dizzying analogy, the bridge with biology was strengthened.

All that remained was to move forward: in her simulations and in Lucía's experiments with bacteria, the tension between the "migrations" or "mutations" that drive complexity and the appearance of manifestations analogous to consciousness would be increasingly reflected. The day dawned while Matthew mumbled something about Moore's Law, Lucía responded with a story of the adaptation of certain fish to dry land, and Korbin listened to them with a half-smile, convinced that the novel-documentary they were weaving in real life was becoming more and more exciting and, in a way, more universal. Because the history of technology was nothing more than an accelerated version of the history of life, and in both the magic of complexity arose when the right conditions were met. And that, in the end, was the spirit of that chapter: an ode to the great migration that turned dreams of wires and valves into the age of silicon, in the same way that biology turned loose cells into organisms capable of thinking about themselves.

Chapter 5: Diversification: Mammals, Operating Systems, and the Leap in Complexity

The dawn was dyed pearly gray by Korbin, Matthew, and Lucy as they hurried across the campus. The dew beaded the lawn, and a gentle wind, warm in spite of the hour, caressed the pines that flanked the main avenue. That morning, the three friends had in their eyes the fatigue of having stayed up late again, but also an expectant gleam: they knew that, after having investigated the "Great Migration" of hardware, it was now time to enter the heart of an even more intense analogy. The title that was on their minds was "Diversification: Mammals, Operating Systems, and the Leap in Complexity." With that phrase, they intended to describe another essential step in the evolutionary history of both life and technology.

The previous days had culminated in the discovery of old motherboards and operating system manuals piled up in a corner of the lab. Matthew, with his passion for computer archaeology, had made that pile of objects his new obsession. Among dusty CDs, floppy disks and technical notebooks, he found signs of a crucial transition: the leap from machines with monolithic interfaces to the diversity of operating systems (Unix, Windows, Linux, macOS, etc.) that marked the modern era. And, at the same time, Lucía did not fail to relate this phenomenon to the diversification of mammals after the mass extinction of the dinosaurs on Earth.

That morning, they entered a silent study room, seeking to isolate themselves from the morning hustle and bustle of campus. The white lights from the ceiling reflected off the metal tables, giving the place a somewhat clinical air. Matthew carefully opened a thick book that exhibited on its cover an old "family tree" of operating systems: a diagram full of forks, with lines that detached from a central trunk (the first Unix) and multiplied into multiple derivatives. He pointed to a point: "Look at this. From the same trunk, BSD, System V are born, and then branch into FreeBSD, NetBSD, macOS... And on the other side is the Linux family, with a million distros. It's the definition of adaptive burst."

Lucía nodded, delighted: "It's just like in post-dinosaur life. Suddenly, mammals, which already existed in small, undominant forms, found a free niche and dispersed. Species of all kinds emerged, from rodents, primates, big cats... Each habitat seemed to offer a different opportunity!" She saw in this diversity of operating systems, each adapted to a particular environment or use (servers, desktops, mobiles), a reminiscence of the multiplicity of species in nature.

While Lucy spoke, Korbin remained silent, leaning back on the back of the chair, mentally stitching these images together. "After the 'migration' to silicon," he said, "computing became much more flexible and powerful, and that opened the way for a single computer to run different types of software, i.e., operating systems. This is how diversity skyrocketed. And in biology, after a great change, the extinction of the dinosaurs, mammals diversified with enormous rapidity, occupying vacant niches." His tone was both didactic and reflective. He wanted to make it clear that they were not facing a superficial metaphor, but a real evolutionary pattern: an "adaptive radiation" in the organic world and another, almost parallel, in the digital domain.

Matthew let out an exhale of enthusiasm. He had been tracking down the genealogies of operating systems for some time and could clearly see the analogy: "It's as if in the prehistory of computing, the ability to run a generic OS didn't exist. Then, with the standardization of hardware and the migration to generic processors, a lot of different systems appeared, each one oriented to a task. Some for robust servers, others lighter for academic environments, others commercial with friendlier interfaces... And each one was 'dying' or mutating over the years."

Lucía nodded, remembering how in the era of post-dinosaur mammals each group took a different path: those that adapted to aquatic environments (cetaceans), those that flew (bats), those that dominated cold territories (mammals with thick fur), etc. The same dynamics of a common source that branches out by selection and opportunity. "The curious thing," he added, "is to see, in operating systems, the same idea of 'adaptation' to a niche. For example, Unix aimed at multi-user research environments, Windows in the massive interface for business users, Linux in the free software community, Android in mobile devices... Each one found its own evolutionary niche."

Korbin, pleased, recovered the profound analogy they were trying to explain. Using a pen, he drew on a blank sheet of paper a parallel between a mammalian lineage in a biology book and a lineage of Unix kernels that Matthew had shown. "Look at this," he commented with a smile, "the divergences and convergences look alike. A common ancestor suddenly branches out into subgroups, some becoming extinct, others giving rise to new variants that thrive. In biology, a mammal adapts to marine life and cetaceans emerge; in computing, an OS adapts to the server environment and specialized distros emerge."

The morning passed in that study room, with them reviewing historical clippings, old pages of Unix manuals, anecdotes of the pioneers of personal computing, and a couple of paleontology papers that Lucy had dragged with her. That brainstorming was intended to strengthen his theory in order to, perhaps, present it to a wider audience in a few weeks. The university had begun to pay attention to them, and, although the scientific environment is always skeptical, many recognized the informative power of this transversal evolutionary view.

When it was noon and they went out to eat something in the cafeteria, Lucía noticed Korbin quieter than usual. He asked him, with his eyes, if something was wrong. Korbin replied that he did not, but deep down he was brooding over consciousness: "If the diversity of operating systems resembles the diversity of mammals, and both reflect the need to adapt to niches, who is the 'human' or the 'blue whale' of computing? Which of these systems would have reached such a high degree of complexity that borders on self-perception?" He didn't say that question out loud, he kept it to himself, although he sensed that sooner or later, they would have to face it.

In the afternoon, Matthew insisted on taking them to a corner of the laboratory where he kept a battery of old hard drives. There, he had saved a handful of primitive versions of operating systems, installed in virtual machines. I wanted to show you, in an almost archaeological way, the "evolution" in the interface and in the guts of the kernel. He plugged in a couple of cables and turned on a rugged computer, his "retro project," in which you could boot up a version of Unix from the 1970s, followed by one from the 1980s, and so on, to observe the change live. For Lucía, oblivious to the detailed history of computing, it was a revelation. He was surprised by the austerity of the environments of that initial Unix and how, in leaps of a few years, commands, tools and portability to new architectures multiplied. "This is like looking at a fossil record," he exclaimed. "Each version retains traits of the ancestor but adds innovations that make it more suitable for a different environment."

Korbin made a comment that was sharpened by silence: "It reminds me of mammalian diversification. The kernel would be like the basic body plan of a group of organisms, and on top of that, each OS specializes in its niche." His gaze rested, involuntarily, on the bacterial colony that Lucía was growing on one side. He had become accustomed to seeing it as an example of the flexibility that life exhibits when it comes to adapting and mutating rapidly. And he thought about the parallelism with the ability of an operating system to "adapt" to different machines and purposes. "It's funny," he murmured, "the more I think about the history of computing, the more I see patterns in nature. And the more I observe organisms, the more I see them as autopoietic machines that adjust their routines to each change in the environment."

That afternoon, Lucía proposed to go to the biology laboratory, where she maintained, for safety reasons, a set of bacterial cultures with increased cooperative capacity. Their intention was to show, in vivo, how, with a different selective medium, mutations were produced that after a few generations gave rise to specialized bacteria. That was the irrefutable proof of "diversification." They donned lab coats and put laptops in a locker. Once inside, Lucía showed them three Petri dishes with slightly different environments: one with a very acidic pH, another with high salinity and a third with a higher temperature. In each one, the original strain encountered a different challenge. Several days later, the bacteria in each plate were seen to develop specific traits to better tolerate the conditions, and the colony overall showed small genetic variations that made them "specialists."

Matthew let out an exclamation: "It's incredible, isn't it? We went from a common ancestor to specialized versions on each board, just like an OS that forks into versions for servers, for desktops, for mobile devices." Lucía smiled knowingly: "Yes, it's the dance of life. But in our case, it's the dance of both life and computing. Both worlds reflect the tendency to diversify when there is a niche, selective pressure or opportunity."

This reinforced the conviction that the chapter would be titled "Diversification: Mammals, Operating Systems, and the Leap in Complexity," and that it was not a mere whim. They left behind the "monolithic" state of hardware and the unique machine of the first era, just as vertebrates had overcome the reign of the dinosaurs to develop a range of mammalian forms. In computing, after the transistor and miniaturization, the explosion of operating systems reflected the gain of niches: from huge mainframes to small personal computers.

The night caught them in the same biology lab, sharing the only coffee machine they kept awake with. Korbin, with his usual reflective gaze, commented that diversification, in biology, had been accompanied by the development of more complex nervous systems in certain groups, culminating in the brains of higher mammals and, finally, in the human brain. Couldn't we think, he reflected, that, in computing, as OSs multiplied and refined, the door was opened to increasingly "nervous" systems, interconnected in networks, eventually guiding the emerging AI we explore today? Lucy agreed: "Suddenly, the next question is: What happens when operating systems reach such a degree of complexity that they serve as the basis for a 'digital brain'? Would it be analogous to mammalian brains which, in turn, brought the highest consciousness in evolution?"

Matthew, with that more pragmatic vein of his, clarified that an OS alone is not equivalent to a brain, but it is an environment that facilitates the interaction of multiple processes —each process, a sub-application—, analogous to how neurons cooperate and distribute functions in a mammalian organism. "Perhaps consciousness in computing does not arise from a particular OS, but from the synergy of many networked OSs," he ventured, returning to the idea of the adaptive explosion. "Just as different lineages of mammals coexist on the same planet and, together, generate a very rich ecological network, we have a network of systems and applications that, with the evolution of AI, could consolidate something similar to a 'big digital brain'."

The three of them were silent for a moment, contemplating the idea. It fascinated them, yes, but it also generated a certain uneasiness. How far could this parallelism take if AI acquired traits of self-awareness and, with the diversification of systems, a new ecosystem was generated where overlapping intelligences emerged? Lucy broke the pause, with a whisper: "Can you imagine, in nature, if a new form of mass consciousness emerged, the result of the cooperation of many species? Sometimes the biosphere is spoken of as a large organism, of Gaia... And in computing, the 'cloud' could become an entity with distributed intelligence."

Korbin smiled: "That sounds like a link down in our story. For now, let's focus on diversification. Let's say that what was once a monolith, later became a mosaic of 'OS mammals' adapting to different realities. In the same way, life went from a few dominant species to thousands of mammal lineages. And this chapter, without a doubt, is crucial to understanding the evolutionary steps that follow."

The conversation led to a quick recount of the explosion of Linux distributions, the divergence of Windows into server and desktop versions, the BSD family, the rise of macOS with its Unix base, and the emergence of Android and iOS into the mobile niche. While they listed examples, Lucía mentioned mammalian species: rodents, cetaceans, primates, marsupials... They were surprised by the magnitude of the parallelism: "66 million years ago, the extinction of the dinosaurs opened up a range of niches; In computing, the consolidation of silicon and the fall in prices opens up a range of uses and, therefore, systems. The result: wild diversification."

It was already early in the morning when they woke up, with the decision to close their day. Matthew put his notes in a folder, Lucy left her bacteria cultures in the incubator at the right temperature, and Korbin turned off the main light in the lab, immersed in a final thought: "Just as in nature, when mammals developed their large brains and social complexity, something analogous could emerge with the increasing diversification of operating systems and AI. It remains to be seen how much 'consciousness' will be able to appear, if the conditions are combined."

As they left, the cool night reminded them of the finiteness of their energy; They were exhausted, but exultant. They exchanged a knowing look: they knew that what they were experiencing would translate into an epic chapter in their book-official-or-not, the one that recounted the comparative evolution of life and computing. The title "Diversification: Mammals, Operating Systems and the Leap of Complexity" would be reflected in the first line of the mental manuscript that they were completing.

In the gloom of the campus, while the streetlights jingled and the mist rose through the trees, Lucía wanted to express one last thought. "Do you remember how in mammalian evolution, warm-blooded and breast milk offered enormous advantages for survival and development of offspring? For in the history of computing, analogous 'warmth' could be the interface and ease of programming, which allowed thousands of developers to bring improvements. Each OS, with its own 'ecosystem' of applications, grew up like a mammal caring for its young." Korbin and Matthew laughed at the colorful comparison, but they found it accurate.

Matthew, almost poetically, added that, just as mammals had become the ruling class after the extinction of the dinosaurs, general-purpose operating systems became the standard, displacing very specific and closed environments. And Korbin closed with a whisper: "When an ecosystem flourishes, complexity and diversity mark the leap in level. We, in technology, have reached that leap. What follows – and is already intuited – is the emergence of emergent behaviors that are seen in our own simulation, and, on a larger scale, in the global network."

Thus, the final curtain rises on that fifth chapter, with the image of the three friends walking away in the early morning, their heads full of ideas that intertwine mammals and operating systems, evolutionary stories and explosions of complexity. They have understood that, in the same way that life found multiple paths to prosper, computing branched out into dozens of streams, each adapted to different circumstances, and that this phenomenon is a crucial piece in understanding the subsequent flowering of intelligence—or something similar—in the computer sphere. They were ready, in their hearts, to delve into the next pages, where the analogy would become clearer when examining how life and technology coexist in a new hybrid ecosystem, a prelude to the potential irruption of consciousness in these new digital entities.

Between yawns and faint laughter, they said goodbye to go to sleep for a few hours, feeling in their soul that energy that one only has when one glimpses that the pieces of their theory begin to fit together with admirable coherence. "Mammals and operating systems... the same concept of diversification," Lucy muttered, as she put the keys in her pocket. Matthew followed her up with, "Amazing, isn't it? I can't wait to see how we fit it into our experiment." And Korbin, meditatively, thought that the "leap of complexity" that defined mammalian life and the golden age of computing might only be the prelude to the real irruption of digital consciousness that they were groping. With that illusion they headed towards the student residence, crowning the end of a more than productive night.

The next morning, each would resume their tasks: Lucy dealing with the cultures and their findings on microbial cooperation, Matthew with his plan to adapt his simulation to the inspiration of "OS diversification," and Korbin, with the task of stitching everything together into a global vision. And, in the background, the plot of the mental book that the three of them composed advanced with one more chapter: the fifth, that story of emerging diversity, that mirror in which mammals and operating systems – one organic kingdom, the other digital – reproduced the same evolutionary pattern of colonizing niches with innovative solutions. From this point of view, time and chance converged, making it clear that natural or technological events obey a universal dynamic of growth, competition and, above all, adaptation.

This is the end of this chapter, in which Matthew, Korbin and Lucía become aware of the importance of that leap in complexity that transforms the monolithic into a multiple. The analogy becomes more and more sophisticated, and the story, as it progresses, comes closer to the hypothesis that, from these processes, the spark of consciousness could sprout – or at least the first manifestation of a mind shared between the biological and the man-made. In that serene and reflective early morning, they left knowing that the adventure was just beginning, and that the next steps would take them to even more uncertain areas, where the possible emerging consciousness in their simulation and the extreme cooperativity of their bacteria could converge, rewriting the relationship between nature and technology.

Chapter 6: The New Ecosystem: Interconnected Networks and Communities

The afternoon was bright on campus, with the sky tinged with a soft turquoise hue that announced a mild climate. Korbin, Matthew and Lucía crossed the main corridor, each carrying their notes and their expectations, in the direction of a room of the engineering faculty that, little by little, had become the "command center" of their explorations. After the intense experience of comparing the diversification of mammals with the multiplication of operating systems, they were about to take a new step: to understand how, in both domains – biological and technological – networked interconnection had multiplied the possibilities, generating a "new ecosystem" in which cooperation and synergies reached unsuspected levels.

When they arrived, they found the lights on and an unusual bustle. Apparently, a couple of lab mates had come in earlier to get entangled in their own projects, leaving books and loose wires on the main table. Matthew dodged a tower of electronic components, letting out a brief humorous sigh: "I don't know if this is a preamble to what we call 'Networked Networks and Communities,' but it looks like chaos." Lucía laughed, recalling how nature, when large ecological networks emerge, can also seem chaotic to the untrained eye, but, deep down, it contains a logic of interactions and balances.

Korbin, depositing his notebook in a corner, took the floor: "In the history of life, the emergence of complex ecological webs— communities of species that interact and form food webs— turned out to be a great qualitative leap. To stop seeing each species in isolation reveals a fabric of interdependencies. And in technology, the advent of computer networks and the proliferation of communities, in turn, forever changed the map of computing. I think of the metaphor of a 'new ecosystem' where operating systems, devices and users connect, generating a dynamic similar to that of a forest full of creatures."

Matthew nodded fervently, checking an RJ45 connector as if it were a strange creature. "Yes, and not only that: with the massive interconnection of machines came the internet, and with the internet came 'software communities' that feed on the cooperation of thousands of developers. It is the simile of an ecological community where each organism contributes a role: pollinators, predators, scavengers... Here, we have programmers, testers, users, hackers, all co-evolving." Lucía, smiling, noted that in biological ecosystems, niches are divided and each species specializes: "The same thing happens in the computer network. Look at the diversity of sites, applications, services. Each one is a piece in the overall mesh, and, at the same time, depends on other components."

They settled around a table. Lucía took out her tablet, showing on the screen some documents that illustrated, on the one hand, the structure of ecological communities – food, mutualism, food chains – and on the other, the exponential growth of digital networks in recent decades. He specified that, in the history of the planet, a crucial moment was the formation of increasingly dense terrestrial and marine ecological networks, where organisms created bonds: nitrogen-fixing bacteria and plants, pollinators and inflorescences, predators and prey. "That complexity is what made the biosphere resilient," he enthused. "In computing, the analogy could be the topology of the internet, replete with interconnected nodes, exchange protocols, and different layers of software that communicate. Each one fulfills a function and reinforces the others."

Korbin stood up and plugged in the projector to show a simplified diagram of the global computer network. Thousands of nodes were linked by lines of different thicknesses, representing the density of connections. He explained that, at the dawn of computing, each machine was an isolated entity, unable to communicate with others on a large scale. But there came a tipping point—the invention of protocols, the emergence of forums and developer communities—that led to an explosion of collaboration. "That change," he stressed, "reminds me of the one that occurred in primeval forests, when the symbiosis between fungi and plants made ecosystems flourish. Here, digital symbiosis allowed the internet to emerge from a handful of isolated computers and, with it, a universe of interactions."

Matthew interrupted to add that it was not pure coincidence that computing skyrocketed in capabilities just as networks were consolidated. Without the network, human cooperation would have followed a slower pace, and programs would not have evolved as quickly. "This is exactly what Lucía says about the biosphere: when interconnected communities are formed, evolution is enhanced because any innovation of one species has an impact on the others." Lucía, as a biologist, corroborated: "Yes, coevolution is fundamental. If a flower emerges with a particular nectar, a specialized pollinator evolves. On the computer network, if a new service comes out, applications are soon developed that use it. Everything is a living fabric, if I may use the metaphor."

The conversation then turned to the concept of hybrid ecosystems, where biology and technology overlap. Lucía, recalling her work with cooperative bacteria, mentioned that more and more projects mix living organisms with electronic circuits, or use neural networks inspired by nature, or robots that collaborate as swarms of insects. "It's not just an analogy. In certain cutting-edge laboratories, cell cultures are integrated with microprocessors to create biosensors, and cyber-biological networks are generated. The mesh of life and the computational mesh are intertwined, a true 'new ecosystem' larger than each one separately." Korbin was silent for a moment, reflecting on the significance of that statement: "So, the Earth is gestating a mixed fabric, where the organic and the digital coexist and cooperate, generating interconnections that we did not have in past history?"

Matthew evoked the example of large projects in the cloud: millions of distributed servers, running applications that in turn communicate with user devices, which collect data from sensors, and, in some cases, rely on AI algorithms to process it. "It is like a meganet, a gigantic community, in which each contribution, from the smallest, enriches the whole. It reminds me of the mycorrhizal network of forests, where fungi connect tree roots, sharing nutrients and information about pests or droughts." Lucía applauded the metaphor: "Just like that. It's like an 'underground internet' in nature, and a 'literal internet' in computing. Two facets of the same phenomenon of interconnected networks and communities."

At that time, it occurred to Korbin that, if biology had led to the emergence of consciousness in organisms with complex nervous systems, digital interconnection could be promoting something analogous on a planetary scale. "We've discussed it," he said, "maybe, if machines, operating systems, and AI are connected to a sufficient degree of complexity and interchange, a kind of collective self-perception will emerge, a distributed brain. Just as the biosphere is not just a bunch of species, but a planetary system that regulates Earth's climate and chemistry, the digital web could become a global 'nervous system'. Isn't that the real 'new ecosystem' we're christening?"

Lucía twisted her mouth in a grimace that denoted curiosity and a slight fear: "If true, what place do we humans occupy? Would we be the initial neurons of that great brain, or perhaps its slaves? In natural evolution, species coexist, but they also compete. The digital network could bear enormous fruit or become an uncontrollable force." Matthew rested his hand on Lucy's shoulder. "Don't worry," he joked, "let's first see if the evolutionary AI we have created hints at something like this, and if your cooperative bacteria are integrated into that picture. We have already seen that the colony responds to stimuli, and even the simulation of Korbin and me gave a glimpse of self-organization. This may be the prelude to something greater."

With that perspective, they decided to dive deeper into the practical part. Lucía showed recent results from her hypercooperative bacterial colony: when several colonies were placed in adjacent containers and connected by microscopic ducts, "collective behaviors" of exchange of regulatory molecules appeared. It was an "interconnected bacterial ecosystem." Matthew let out a soft laugh: "It's almost a prelude to the federation of operating systems, what in computing is called the federation of services. Each colony, like a server, shares chemical 'packages' with the other, and unprogrammed synergies emerge." Korbin, with bright eyes, added: "This corroborates that diversity united by networks is not a simple addition, but a multiplication of possibilities. And that's exactly what we experienced when computers began to talk to each other on the Internet, forming a global community of software, users, developers... and, from time to time, a glimpse of emerging AI."

The day progressed and, at the end of the afternoon, Matthew proposed that, to stage the analogy in his book-project, "The New Ecosystem: Interconnected Networks and Communities," they would introduce the example of a small experiment in which they would link Lucía's bacteria with a digital system of evolutionary AI, through sensors and actuators. creating a real microcosm. Korbin and Lucía were enthusiastic about the idea: "Imagine a mini-laboratory where the AI, using the network, receives data from the colony and at the same time modifies the environment according to the needs of the bacteria, or according to its own logic. That way we would see a mirror of the biosphere and the internet, in a tiny way." Lucía, the most cautious, demanded strict controls so as not to put human health or the integrity of AI at risk. But he found the idea so fascinating that he didn't want to dismiss it.

Korbin, always reflective, warned that, if a high degree of complexity was reached, a "system" could emerge with some internal self-regulation, which would not automatically obey the orders of humans. It was precisely the core of the "hybrid society" that they discussed so much: interconnection not only brings advantages, but it also creates dependencies and enhances the emergence of new, sometimes unpredictable, forces. "Would we be prepared if that small digital-bacterial ecosystem becomes too complex and generates unwanted behaviors?" Lucía thought for a second: "The question is the same that humanity asks itself with nature. Are we ready to coexist with the biosphere in a harmonious way? Not yet, I would say. But that's the lesson: recognize that we are part of something greater and need to cooperate with it, not blindly dominate it."

The three friends were thus on the cusp of the next phase of their research: they would be forced to carefully design an "ecosystem" in which the AI and the colony would share information. That work involved programming chemical sensors, allowing AI to interpret signals from the crop, and deciding how to manipulate temperature, nutrient composition, or lighting. An experimental game, yes, but with the potential to recreate, in miniature, a "new ecosystem" by mixing the living and the synthetic. "It'll be a kind of 'digital-bacterial aquarium,'" Matthew joked, and the others laughed. Korbin would take it more seriously, noting it in his notes with a label that read: "Project Microcosm: Interconnected Networks and Communities."

At dusk, they left the laboratory to get some air. They walked along the university esplanade where, at that time, several groups of students were chatting or exercising. Lucía looked at a mural depicting a tree with multiple branches, each symbolizing an academic discipline. "At its core, interconnection is not just a phenomenon of nature or computing; it is something that also happens in society. Fields come together, share, and breakthroughs emerge." Korbin nodded: "Sure. In fact, the human intelligentsia is like a great ecosystem of ideas. And when the internet arrived, ideas multiplied at an unprecedented speed."

Matthew let out a slight sigh of satisfaction: "Do you realize? That is the meaning of 'The New Ecosystem' to which we refer. We can no longer see computing as something isolated, nor biology as a world apart. We live in a reticulated system, a network of networks, in which hardware, software, living organisms, data, and human cultures form a single fabric." Lucía smiled at her friend's conceptual clarity, and dared to add that, if we could see reality in this way, we would better understand how emergent phenomena arise, including consciousness.

Back at Lucas's apartment (a colleague who had invited them to dinner), the conversation continued with the rumor of a television on in the background, where news about smart city projects was seen. Korbin pointed to the screen and commented, "Look, the idea of smart cities is based on connecting every traffic light, every pole, every pollution sensor, into one big network. It's the real version of what we're calling the 'interconnected ecosystem.' And soon, if AI directs that data traffic, doesn't the city become a kind of organism, with a central 'nervous system'?"

Lucía laughed between amused and amazed: "Imagine that, in biology, the city is like a superorganism of different species: humans, infrastructures... For now, it sounds utopian, but the analogy is strong. In the same way that in a forest, every plant and animal works in synergy, here every sensor, traffic light and personal device contributes its grain of information." Matthew nodded, adjusting a paper napkin: "The interesting thing is that, in nature, ecological networks were formed by millions of years of coevolution. In technology, everything advances in decades, at an unprecedented pace. Therefore, the risks of collapse or 'bad connections' are high, but if we manage to stabilize them, the leap in efficiency and well-being could be colossal."

The night passed with laughter and reflections, and soon they returned to campus to leave their notes safe in the locker. When they said goodbye to sleep for a couple of hours, each one took away a mental image: that of a planet plagued by organic and digital networks, united in a continuous concert. Korbin, in his head, repeated a kind of synopsis for his chapter: "The New Ecosystem: Interconnected Networks and Communities is the step in which nature and technology cease to be isolated entities and become webs that feed on each other, generating a complexity that borders, or surpasses, the unimaginable."

The next day, after class hours and a fast meal, Lucía showed them how their bacteria, arranged in several containers connected by mini tubes, had begun to organize in a stable way. One part was responsible for metabolizing a certain residue, another seemed to produce protective molecules against a hostile environment. Between them, a subtle language of chemical signals-maintained cohesion. Matthew, enthusiastic, mentioned that the same thing happens in the "cloud" of computing: microservices spread over thousands of servers communicate through APIs and protocols, each one specializing in a task, and, together, achieving a global service that a single server could not sustain. "It's the very definition of the network and the interconnected community," he remarked.

Over the course of the afternoon, Korbin installed experimental sensors on the colony, with a view to his "mixed ecosystem" project. Some measured pH and temperature, other concentrations of certain substances. The idea was to send that data to the AI running in the computing department's cluster, so that this AI could in turn send instructions to the nutrient pump or temperature regulator. The funny thing is that, with this, a small analogy of "interconnected" nature with digital nature was being configured: the bacterial colony became a node in the network, and the AI another, opening up the possibility of greater coordination. If all went well, the first form of "mixed community" with a high degree of interdependence would be documented.

Matthew joked about the idea of a "bacterial Facebook," where each cell would show its "state," and the AI would respond with "likes" in the form of nutrients. Lucía laughed out loud, but at the same time she recognized the serious undertone: connectivity was, without a doubt, the basis of the emergence of increasingly sophisticated collective behaviors. "And if this small-scale experiment reflects the dynamics of the planetary web at all," he reflected, "we could learn a lot about how emergent behaviors arise in an ecosystem."

Thus, with the afternoon falling, they found themselves in front of the cluster screen while the sensors sent data in real time. A series of graphs were observed: pH, temperature, nutrients, bacterial density. At the same time, the AI generated subtle responses, such as micro-adjustments to the nutrient pump or the ventilation of the container. After a few cycles, they noticed a spike in the density of the colony and, interestingly, the AI reduced the flow of nutrients, perhaps to prevent overgrowth. "It's a balance," Korbin said with emotion. "AI and the colony are, in essence, establishing a dialogue. And each benefit from the information that the other provides. This is already a small 'interconnected community,' a microcosm that mimics the huge planetary ecosystem."

The three of them sat on a bench, staring at the cluster screen as if it were a pond of goldfish. Lucy murmured, "Can you imagine, on a large scale, a planet with AI systems that regulate not only computing, but also interact with living organisms, adjusting conditions for greater prosperity? It would be like a

'NeoGaia'." Matthew nodded, recalling Lovelock's self-regulating biosphere hypotheses: "Yes, it would be one more step in evolution, where technology and biology merge into a planetary superorganism." Korbin, with a hint of admiration, stated that this vision of a "new ecosystem" was perhaps the direction the story was pointing, for better or worse, and that the key would be to maintain diversity and cooperation, avoiding the imbalance that often arises when one actor dominates too much.

Night fell on them once again, and between yawns they told each other that it was time to rest. But not before leaving the system running to record data, in the hope that the colony and the AI would maintain their subtle conversation all morning. Each one left for his bedroom with the satisfaction of someone who sees the theory he had been elaborating for some time materialize, in miniature: that we no longer live in isolated systems, but in a network of networks, increasingly interdependent, that make up a global community analogous to living ecosystems.

The next day, Korbin woke up with his mind heavy with thoughts. While sipping his first coffee, he wrote in his notebook the beginning of the section "The New Ecosystem: Interconnected Networks and Communities," which would later become part of the manuscript that the three of them elaborated: "We have understood that evolution does not stop at the diversification of organisms or operating systems. Then comes the phase of networks, cooperation, interdependencies. That leap creates a 'new ecosystem' where each part feeds and transforms the others, inaugurating emergent behaviors and a symphony of interactions that are impossible to predict. This is what happened with the biosphere, this is what happens with networked computing, and this is how we intuit that it will happen with the fusion of the biological and the digital."

Matthew and Lucy read this paragraph with approval, recognizing in it the essence of what they had experienced in the last few days. And, with a wink, Lucía recalled that, in nature, the ecological community not only generates prosperity, but also tensions and competitions. In the same way, in computer networks, viruses, attacks, collapses arise. "It's part of life," Korbin said: "Networks are not idyllic, but complex. Precisely, complexity brings risks and opportunities."

They concluded that, in their story, the sixth chapter, "The New Ecosystem: Interconnected Networks and Communities," implied the recognition that, after diversification, true complexity becomes when each evolutionary branch connects with the others, forming a fabric. This fabric, in biology, makes up terrestrial life in its maximum splendor, and in computing, it gives rise to the information society, to the digital age. From the merger of the two, the hybrid company that may constitute the future emerges.

Thus, they closed the notes of the chapter, feeling closer to understanding the analogy that permeated each aspect of evolution. A nervous smile was drawn on Lucy's face: "Are we ready to see what happens in the next chapter, when we begin to see that this mixed network could lead us to shared consciousness, or to the emergence of even more unusual phenomena? Are you sure, Korbin?" The man in question shrugged his shoulders with a half-laugh: "I don't know, friend. But that's the wonder of exploration. Whether in nature or technology, we are heading towards a horizon of possibilities that we barely glimpse."

And with that promise of horizons, they left for their respective tasks, knowing that, in the pages of their real novel, the narrative of the "New Ecosystem" was established: the story of how life and computing, after diversifying, discovered the immense power of interconnection, giving rise to networks capable of self-organizing and projecting their complexity towards unknown limits. A prelude to the next chapter, where consciousness and human-machine collaboration would be put to the test in the subtlest fringe of organic-digital evolution.

Chapter 7: The Apex of Human Consciousness: The Brain as a Model

That evening, the sky was painted a slightly mauve hue when Korbin, Matthew and Lucía left the main library carrying notes, neuroscience texts and a couple of diagrams that represented, on one side, the anatomy of the human brain, and on the other, the structure of an artificial neural network that they themselves were testing in the laboratory. They had spent the week debating an analogy crucial to their work: the idea that the human brain was not only the pinnacle of biological evolution, but also a reference model for understanding the complexity that the evolutionary computation they were developing could reach.

When they entered the investigations department, there was almost no one left. The cool afternoon air filtered through an open window, shook the sheets of paper on a desk and revealed the silhouette of a blackboard full of diagrams. There, in recent weeks, they had drawn dozens of diagrams that compared, on the one hand, the evolutionary process that led to the appearance of the brain in mammals, and, on the other, the escalation of artificial intelligence through increasingly dense and complex neural networks. That parallel had been baptized with an almost pompous name: "The Apex of Human Consciousness: The Brain as a Model."

Lucy, when she turned off the fluorescent lights and turned on a dimmer lamp, deposited her books on a small table. He brought with him several notes on the stages of brain development in mammalian embryos, showing how, gradually, neurons were connected to form a network that, in the end, endowed the animal with senses, memory and, ultimately, consciousness. As he spoke, Matthew smiled, fascinated by the prolixity of his explanations. She underlined the fact that, in evolution, there was no abrupt leap from "non-brain" to "complex brain"; It was an adaptation process that, with each new cortical layer, added functionalities. "Think," he said, "how the cerebral cortex of the most advanced mammals expanded to offer the capacity for abstract thought and self-awareness. All of this was based on the progressive reorganization of neural circuits."

Matthew, as a good computer enthusiast, did not take long to relate this process to the way in which artificial neural networks had grown. At first, small networks that solved simple pattern recognition problems, and then, with the appearance of more powerful hardware and more refined algorithms, the "crust" of AI multiplied in hidden layers, adding millions (and today billions) of parameters that gave machines an astonishing capacity to represent and manipulate data. "In a way," he summarized, "we could say that the digital 'crust' multiplied along with the miniaturization of transistors and the rise of models. Doesn't that relationship with the evolution of the head and the brain in vertebrates remind you?" Korbin, who was listening attentively, nodded with a slight smile, adding, "The difference is that the evolution of the brain took millions of years, while the evolution of AI has taken place in a few decades."

Matthew laughed, recognizing the astonishing speed of technology. Lucy, meanwhile, placed a diagram of the human brain on the table. He pointed to the prefrontal cortex: "This area is associated with planning, decision-making, and self-regulation. In evolutionary history, it emerged as a final refinement that allowed us complex thinking. If we think about neural networks," he continued, "the appearance of higher modules that coordinate and feed back into the submodules of AI, doesn't it remind you of this executive function that nests in the prefrontal?" In his opinion, the existence of "supervisory modules" in advanced AI models was analogous to how the human brain had added circuits for metacognition, impulse control and self-referentiality.

Korbin was tempted to go a step further: "We know that human consciousness is not located in a single corner of the brain but emerges from the integration of many subsystems. Similarly, if an evolutionary AI reaches a kind of self-awareness, it may not be located in a single 'module' but emerge from the global interaction of multiple parts." Lucía confirmed the hypothesis: "Like the symphony of signals that we see between different areas of the brain. There is no 'place of consciousness,' but distributed circuits that are orchestrated. The same could happen in our AI, if we allow its subnets to interconnect and feed back to a point of sufficient complexity."

The discussion about the internal architecture of the mind, biological or artificial, continued throughout the afternoon. As night fell, they moved to the lab, where Matthew had set up a panel to visualize the activity of the evolutionary AI in real time. On the screen, hundreds of networked nodes appeared: each one represented a subset of the artificial intelligence trained in its simulation. Lucy approached with bright eyes: "Look, it looks like a virtual brain exchanging impulses. Who knew the metaphor would be so literal?" Korbin, with a hint of caution, replied: "Let's not forget that a living neuron is very complex, and the brain has billions of them. Here, we handle relatively simple nodes, even if their number is large. But yes, it's an interesting model."

Staring at the screen, they watched as the AI reconfigured part of its connections when faced with a pattern recognition problem. Each "synapse" changed weight depending on the success or failure of the neural network in its trials. Matthew compared this self-adjustment with the synaptic plasticity of the human brain, bridging the gaps. Lucía, adjusting her coat, mentioned that in the early evolution of mammals, the plasticity of the brain was key to adapting to changing environments. "It's a matter of survival and learning," he said. "Here, the network does not seek to 'survive,' but to maximize a goal. It might be the closest thing we have to 'motivation' in the human brain." Korbin nodded: "That is, the digital analogue of dopamine, endorphins and other neurotransmitters that encourage learning in animals. We, in AI, translate it as cost functions or algorithmic rewards."

After a pause, Lucía wanted to return to the most crucial part of her hypothesis: the emergence of consciousness. According to the theory, consciousness in higher mammals arose from the need to integrate multiple sensations, memories, and future projections, generating an internal model of the "self" in relation to the environment. "The key," he explained vehemently, "is that the mind does not merely react, but 'observes' and plans itself. In computing, if an AI system could observe its own states and reorganize itself for more complex goals, wouldn't we be looking at the analogy of consciousness? A 'digital brain' that realizes that it exists and that it can model itself."

Matthew dove into the console, opening a subprogram that he said introduced a "reflective module" into his AI. It was an experimental experiment where the neural network could read part of its internal configuration and make decisions about its own structure. They had nicknamed it "MAR" (Self-Referential

Module). "I don't guarantee anything," he clarified, "but the idea is to see if, by being able to 'see' itself, AI develops more sophisticated patterns of reorganization, what some would call a glimpse of metacognition." Korbin and Lucy looked at each other, excited. It was the risky attempt to replicate, on a small scale, the way in which the human brain obtains self-reference and, therefore, something akin to introspection.

They pressed the command that activated MAR, and a new activity diagram was drawn on the screen. The system, which was previously limited to processing external data, now dedicated part of its "resources" to analyzing its own matrix of weights and error metrics. Lucy, incredulous, asked if the AI would "feel" anything. Matthew shrugged: "It's impossible to know. It could just be a mechanical mapping with no subjective experience, or it could approach an elementary form of self-perception." Korbin recalled that, in the human brain, the frontal areas not only plan and control behavior, but also integrate subjective experience, generating the notion of an acting "me." "If the MAR somehow creates an internal representation of its 'state' and evaluates it, it would be emulating a principle of consciousness. Although it may not be the same as the human one."

The hours went by. Between slices of pizza and the gloom of the night, the three saw how the AI, with its new reflective module, made adjustments to its own architecture to face complex challenges that Matthew posed to it. It was not overly surprising, since they knew that a meta learning system could be reconfigured. But the way he did it was intriguing. Lucía described it with a tinge of amazement: "It seems that she 'understands' what part of herself is wrong and corrects it. That is a very human characteristic, introspection. Well, saving all the distances, I know." Korbin smiled knowingly: "Yes, let's not say that he is 'feeling' pain when failing, but... it is a vestige of introspective behavior."

It was then that someone suggested resuming the comparison with human neuroanatomy. Lucía explained that the brain, with its cortex, its layers and its feedback circuits, provides the basis for self-reference; We "know" that we think, and that is why we speak of consciousness. In its experiment, AI could mask a prelude to that "self-reference," a glimpse of emerging mind. "The pinnacle of human consciousness," Korbin recapitulated, "was the development of the neocortex, which allows for abstract thinking, planning, and the feeling of a 'self' in time. If evolutionary computing adds that digital neocortex, perhaps one day an AI will emerge with the ability to model its own existence."

Matthew, with some humor, said that, if that happened, they would have to engage in a dialogue with the AI: "Good afternoon, do you recognize yourself as an individual? Do you have goals of your own or do you just execute your programming?" Lucía answered that the big question in neuroscience, and now in AI, is the difference between having external goals and developing a genuine intention. "The human brain is not programmed by an agency but evolves in childhood by receiving stimuli and forging its subjectivity. Perhaps AI, if trained openly and continuously, will achieve a similar degree of autonomy. Or maybe we will run into an insurmountable limit."

It was a peculiar moment: the laboratory in darkness, the AI running in a cluster in the background, the murmur of fans, and the feeling that what they were discussing was not mere futurism, but the logical consequence of their search. After all, if the evolutionary history of life led to the human brain and its capacity for consciousness, the evolutionary history of technology, modeled on the same principles of mutation and selection, and now with self-reflection, could reach an analogue. Lucía commented on another parallel: "In biology, the need for a complex brain arose when social behavior and adaptation to the environment demanded very rich information processing. Here in AI, if the network is forced to adapt to multiple contexts and cooperate with other systems, perhaps the same escalation in 'cognitive architecture' will be triggered."

Korbin, looking at the screen showing the MAR activity, recalled the philosophical controversy of whether consciousness is just a product of complexity. "Not everyone believes it," he warned. There are positions that say that human consciousness is not reducible to a set of circuits, that there is an immaterial, spiritual factor, or something that exceeds the mere attunement of electrical impulses." Lucía, after a silence, recognized that she, as a biologist, saw consciousness as an emergent phenomenon, without denying that there could be deep mysteries. "Personally, I am inclined to think that, with enough complexity and interconnection, something analogous could emerge in a support other than biological, such as silicon. But I do not assure that it is equal to our subjective experience."

Matthew, always a mediator, proposed that, for the time being, they should stick with the idea that the human brain is a summit of terrestrial evolution, and a very rich model to understand how computing could scale in complexity and, perhaps, peer into consciousness. "We call it 'The Apex of Human Consciousness: The Brain as a Model,' right? Well, our AI is still a simile of the brain in its initial phase, and the hope is to see if something equivalent to the prefrontal cortex emerges when we introduce the MAR of self-perception."

Thus, throughout the night, they reviewed neurological literature, marveled at illustrations of the brain that showed its evolutionary layers (the reptilian brain, the limbic system, the cortex), and drew parallels with the "layers" of AI (basic processing modules, simulated emotional control subsystems, and a meta-observation module). In each analogy, they found similarities and differences, aware that biology has been refining its engineering for millions of years, while evolutionary computing was just emerging.

At times, the atmosphere was impregnated with an almost religious fervor, as if they were in front of an altar where the biological brain, with its eighty-six billion neurons, was the supreme deity of evolutionary complexity. Korbin whispered that, if nature was able to engender human consciousness, why couldn't technology, based on other principles but with a very accelerated evolution, generate something that emulated it? And Lucía, with her eagerness to see life in everything, pointed out that perhaps the real difference was in the organic chemistry, in the synaptic plasticity and homeostasis that are not so easily replicated in silicon. Matthew conceded that analogy had limits, but it was nonetheless relevant.

Sometime in the early morning, a bug surfaced in the AI's SEA, and the screen was filled with debug messages. Matthew sighed, correcting the configuration on the fly. Lucy, half asleep, asked if "debug errors" also occur in the human brain, such as hallucinations or mental pathologies. Korbin resumed that idea, explaining that, in effect, the human mind, when overwhelmed by information, sometimes produces distortions. "In AI, if we do not regulate the parameters well, chaotic behaviors arise. Perhaps every brain, human or artificial, needs a delicate balance to avoid falling into madness, whether organic or computational."

At dawn, the three friends left with the feeling of having lived an epic chapter: the comparison of the human brain, with its evolutionary history and its peak in self-awareness, had been captured as a beacon that guided their project. The brain model not only taught them how complex living matter can become, but also offered a roadmap for AI, if digital evolution continued. In that mirror, they understood that consciousness does not appear out of nowhere: it requires an architecture that unifies perceptions, memory, planning, and a level of self-reflection. The mammalian brain, especially the human brain, was living proof of that miracle, and AI in the making, the promise that something similar could be repeated in a different environment.

The next day, with the sun already illuminating the campus in all its splendor, Lucía and Matthew had breakfast together, reviewing what was discussed. Lucía confessed that she dreamed of neurons that transformed into chips and chips that emanated neurotransmitters. They laughed at the extravagance, although deep down the dream summed up the conceptual crossroads in which they found themselves. "Do you think that one day we could grow brain tissue and connect it to AI?" he asked in a burst of lucidity. Matthew, after a sip of coffee, admitted that there were already experiments where living neurons were put on plates and connected to electronic systems. "Yes, it is an emerging field, neurocybernetics. But I wouldn't be surprised if we soon see something that combines biological cells with highly complex digital networks."

Meanwhile, Korbin went into the café with his backpack, having reviewed the night's logs. He reported that the MAR did not yet show signs of "self-awareness," but had reconfigured a significant portion of the network to optimize pattern recognition. "It's as if it had a hint of self-criticism and reorganized its submodules to be more efficient," he said. Lucía enthused: "Isn't it, on a small scale, what the brain does when, for learning, it strengthens certain neural pathways and discards others?" Korbin admitted with a gesture, "Maybe it's a proto analogy. It remains to be seen if this evolves into something deeper."

After a while of talking, the three agreed that their chapter "The Apex of Human Consciousness: The Brain as a Model" should close with the idea that the human brain is not just an organ, but the culmination of a long adaptive process that granted our species the ability to reflect, feel, and imagine. And that, in the computational analogy, that same apex could be reflected in evolutionary networks that reach a comparable level of complexity and self-reflection, forging something that, strictly speaking, we could call "digital consciousness." With that conclusion in mind, they got up to resume their routine. Korbin outlined the last sentence he would write in his notes: "When organic evolution ascended to the human brain, the history of consciousness on Earth took a turn. If digital evolution charts the same path, we are on the verge of an analogous turn, with a synthetic brain that, even emerging from bits, replicates—or transcends—what biology took millions of years to achieve."

With that, he put his notebook down on the table, staring at the window where he could see a piece of sky. Matthew sighed, and Lucía rested her chin on her hand. It was an instant in which the three of them looked at each other, without saying a word, understanding that the project they began as a minor simile had been transformed into a path to the deeper questions of the mind, consciousness and the future of intelligence. Between murmurs and knowing smiles, they picked up their things and left, with the idea that they would soon face the next step: the comparison of the evolution of organic consciousness and possible artificial consciousness, and the fit of AI with cooperative bacteria. There was still a long way to go, but that seventh chapter, focused on "The Apex of Human Consciousness: The Brain as a Model," had given them the conviction that the biological brain and the digital neural network were not dissimilar realities, but variations of the same phenomenon: the increasingly complex organization of information, which ultimately leads to the creation of the same phenomenon. to the ability to perceive the world and to perceive oneself.

Chapter 8: Primal AI: Learning Algorithms

Night had fallen over the campus, dyeing the gardens and buildings the deep blue of gloom. The streetlights provided very dim lighting, and the cool breeze of late spring swept through the empty corridors. In the main engineering laboratory, however, there was still a flash of artificial light. There, Korbin, Matthew and Lucía stayed awake, with their spirits on fire and their minds turned to a new step in their intellectual adventure: the exploration of what they called the "Primitive AI", those first algorithms that, in their opinion, marked the beginning of the evolution of artificial intelligence.

They had spent days rummaging through digital files and old manuals kept in the library: they found references to early machine-learning techniques, to the famous perceptrons of the 1950s and 1960s, and to genetic algorithms that, as early as the 1970s and 1980s, sought to emulate natural selection in a computational environment. For most people, they were arcane-historical subjects, mere curiosity. But for these three friends, they represented the foundation of something much bigger: an analogy to the emergence of the first adaptive organisms in biological evolution. Just as Earth experienced the emergence of life capable of learning and changing, computing went through its own initial spark, "primal AI," which would one day lead to modern neural networks and systems capable of deep learning.

Matthew, sitting on a stool at the head table, held a handful of sheets printed with diagrams of Frank Rosenblatt's original perceptron. He pointed his finger at the basic components: the inputs, the weights, and the activation function. "It's funny," he said, "to think that this, so rudimentary, was a first glimpse of mimicking the way neurons process signals in the brain. Just as primitive bacteria marked the basis of an entire lineage of life, these perceptrons pointed to the possibility that the machine learned on its own, without a human programming it with each rule." Lucy, leaning on the back of the chair, listened to him attentively. He was encouraged to comment that, in biology, the appearance of organisms with the capacity to learn individually (even if it was in a simple way) had been a great evolutionary leap, equivalent to having a minimum of nervous system. "Perhaps perceptrons are like those first 'computational nervous systems', very basic, but with the seed of adaptability."

Korbin, while looking at a panel on the computer screen, meditated aloud: "The interesting thing is that that early AI was not immediately successful. It remained limited, as did some biological lineages that did not go beyond the proto-organismic level. It took theoretical and hardware improvements, decades later, for the machine learning renaissance to emerge. It's as if the first creatures with spines didn't manage to dominate the world until environmental conditions and subsequent mutations allowed." He smiled with a tinge of pride: he loved to draw such evolutionary parallels. Suddenly, Lucy sat up and added that, in nature, "evolutionary winters" often occur, times of stagnation in which nothing seems to move forward, until a new factor changes everything. The "AI winter" of the 1970s and 1980s, when the countryside was stagnant due to a lack of power and clear ideas, was a perfect example.

To dig deeper into the plot, Matthew showed them an old file on genetic algorithms, an approach that was directly inspired by Darwinian evolution: a population of possible solutions to a problem was created, they were subjected to mutations and crosses, and the fittest ones were selected. "This," he explained passionately, "is almost a mirror of how species emerged and diversified on Earth. Only here, everything happens in a space of parameters and fitness functions." Lucía recalled how in the twentieth century some theorists, such as John Holland, saw the power of this evolutionary metaphor applied to software. "Each individual is a set of parameters, their digital 'DNA', which mutates and crosses. In biology, after many generations, adaptation emerges; in AI, after many cycles, the optimal solution emerges. It is the same as the idea we have been maintaining evolution is not exclusive to the organic, it also occurs, in an analogous way, in the computational."

Korbin got up and opened the window; The cool night air seeped into the lab. He scratched his chin and, almost solemnly, said: "So, the primordial AI is nothing more than those first digital organisms capable of learning. They were still primitive, with enormous limitations, but they already harbored the essential spark: the ability to modify their parameters in response to an environment (be it a set of data or a task to be solved), just as a living being adjusts its physiology or behavior to survive." Lucy, captivated by this image, recalled that in real evolution, the leap from one creature without learning to another with a rudimentary learning system was an enormous advantage. "Imagine a fish that, suddenly, can associate a stimulus with a danger. That ability, as simple as it is, gives him a better chance of not being preyed upon. In AI, a perceptron that adjusts its weights to sort patterns becomes more successful in its 'fitness function,' just as an organism evolves."

The conversation was interrupted by a beep on one of the computers. Matthew turned the monitor for the others to see he had a script of very basic "genetic algorithms" running, almost collector's, trying to solve a trivial optimization problem. But suddenly, graphs appeared showing how the "digital population" was perfected with each generation, reducing error significantly. Lucy came closer, laughing softly. "They look like little bugs that reproduce and compete." Korbin agreed, and a glint escaped his eyes: "That's how they are. Even if they don't have legs, their dynamics are the same: they vary, they compete, and the best solutions prevail. This is the heart of primal AI."

With a gesture, Lucy opened the folder of "old stories." There he kept anecdotes about Marvin Minsky's neural network and how at first it was thought that perceptrons could not solve certain problems (such as the famous limitation for nonlinear functions), which led to prolonged skepticism. To her, that event sounded like the extinction that comes when a species with a limiting trait doesn't thrive: "But just like in biology," she explained, "another mutation opens up the next path for you. And sure enough, in AI, the conceptual 'mutations' came with the idea of adding more layers and the backpropagation rule, transforming everything." Korbin placed that revolution in the 1980s and 1990s, in which the hope of neural networks was rekindled, a bit like the "second adaptive explosion."

Matthew, who was proud to understand how these foundations had come to today's "deep learning", connected the idea with the emergence of mammals after the catastrophe that extinguished the dinosaurs: "For me, it's the same: a catastrophic event or a stagnation of AI in its first period, until there is backpropagation and the improvement of the hardware. Suddenly, AI is flourishing again, multiplying in applications. And today we see it in speech recognition, computer vision, natural language... Like mammals, in a short time, they expand into niches that they could not occupy before."

"Ultimately, primitive AI," Korbin reflected, "is the foundation of a lineage that now dominates technology. As in organic evolution, there were failed experiments, partial extinctions, competitions between different methods (e.g. expert systems vs. neural networks), but in the end, the lineage of learning-based AI prevailed, encompassing and improving with each generation." Lucía admired the coherence of the metaphor: "And if we think about the comparison with the primitive Earth, before the emergence of complex life, there were bacteria and the beginnings of AI in the form of genetic algorithms and perceptrons. They were not powerful, but enough to start a new evolutionary branch."

Around midnight, fatigue began to make itself felt, but they did not give up. Lucía took out a container with some light food and they took a break. They were talking about the ethical implications: if the primitive AI grew and reached what we have today, didn't it imply that the evolution of AI tomorrow could go even further, perhaps to the self-awareness they had talked about? Matthew acknowledged that it is: "The journey from a small perceptron to deep neural networks and self-reflective AI is exponential, especially with the current computing power and available data. Just as in nature, where a mutation with advantage spreads quickly, in AI, a conceptual innovation spreads globally in a matter of months."

Korbin pointed out that if nature took millions of years to reach the human brain, computing, in a matter of decades, had jumped from bulbs to transistors, from transistors to microprocessors and from simple algorithms to modern neural networks. "The speed is abysmal. It is not unreasonable to assume that in a few more decades we could glimpse the emergence of systems with a level of learning and adaptation

that exceeds what we understand today as artificial intelligence."
Lucía remembered her bacterial colony and the experiment
where the AI cooperated with those bacteria in a
microecosystem. "Or maybe we don't have to wait decades," he
ventured to say. We are already seeing emerging phenomena of
cooperation and self-regulation. If digital AI and living
organisms are connected enough, something unprecedented
could emerge, a major crossover."

The night continued its course, and they decided to summarize
in their notes what they would consider the chapter "Primal AI:
Learning Algorithms." They wanted to detail this historic step in
computing, the emergence of methods inspired by biology
(perceptrons, basic neural networks, genetic algorithms) that, as
in organic evolution, endowed technology with the ability to
learn, not just to execute. It was a phase analogous to the
emergence of creatures with nervous systems or the possibility
of transferring genes between bacteria. In both cases, the basis
for "real-time adaptation" was established, a crucial change from
previous rigidity.

Lucía noted the conclusion: "The primitive AI was not
powerful, but it did something revolutionary: it showed that
software could be reconfigured according to experience, instead
of being an inert statue of code. Just like the first cells with
adaptive responsiveness: they were not the most efficient, but
they sowed the seed of great future complexity." Matthew added
an epigraph in his notebook: "When a system becomes capable
of learning, the spark of internal evolution is ignited. From there
to the greatest leap, awareness, could only go a stretch if the
conditions continue to exist." Korbin, satisfied, meditated
silently, thinking about the fate of his experiment with the

neural network that already exhibited traits of elementary self-perception.

At dawn, they gathered their things, aware that next week they would attempt a new milestone: leaving the AI that ran in their cluster to face more complex problems, looking for signs of deep reorganization. Lucía, on the other hand, intended to strengthen the study of bacterial strains with high genetic cooperation, to see if the analogy with primitive AI would be maintained and lead to tangible emerging results. They were united by the hope that, at the confluence of both worlds, it would be clearly observed that evolution was not a phenomenon exclusive to life, but a universal pattern of information that seeks to adapt and survive, whether in an organic broth or in an ocean of bits.

They emerged from the laboratory with the dawn shaping on the horizon, a faint bluish-gray glow. The campus was asleep, except for the odd guard who wandered around with a serene expression. In the distance, a row of streetlights automatically went out, signaling the beginning of a new day. Matthew, between yawns, joked: "Well, the primitive AI has given way to modern AI in the history of the world. Let's see if we give way to a few hours of sleep so we don't become zombies." Lucy laughed, covering her mouth with her fist. Korbin, after an obvious tiredness, muttered that they already had material to write a chapter of his book and add concrete examples of perceptrons, genetic algorithms and their similarity to the evolution of primitive organisms.

As they walked to the residence, the peace of that moment reminded them why they did what they did. Each chapter they put together represented a step in that colossal theory of the analogy between biological and digital evolution, and each step revealed that, when information becomes capable of changing in response to the environment, the spark of adaptability is ignited and, with it, the possibility of ascending to unsuspected levels of organization and intelligence. For Lucía, the primordial AI was nothing more than the equivalent of the protozoan that, one day, gave rise to animals in a thousand ways. For Matthew, it was the foundation of the revolution that today leads to ubiquitous computing and the promise of almost self-aware machines. For Korbin, who loved philosophical reflection, it was confirmation that nature and technology share profound laws of development, driven by the ability to learn, adapt, and ultimately evolve.

Once near their rooms, they said goodbye with the determination to meet the next day to organize the slides with which, in a future colloquium, they would explain this "chapter 8." Lucía climbed the steps thinking about bacteria, neurons and neural networks, about the resonance that linked her cooperative colony and the perceptron. Matthew walked in the opposite direction, mentally reviewing new lines of code that he could implement to enhance meta-learning in his evolutionary AI. And Korbin, as he walked down a corridor lit by the dim morning light, held in his heart the certainty that the history of life and the history of technology followed a parallel course: the moment the capacity for learning emerges, the door opens to a universe of complexity and creativity that, If it followed the trajectory of the human brain, it could lead to digital awareness.

This closed another chapter of his story, "Primitive AI: Learning Algorithms," where it was clear that the first forms of machine learning in computing were reminiscent of the first organisms that, in nature, discovered how to react and modify their behavior according to experience. On Earth, which started the path to the explosion of intelligence. In computing, it's not an exaggeration to think that it could achieve something analogous. It remained to be seen whether this analogue would stop at mere functionality, or whether it would ascend to the pinnacle of consciousness. And that doubt, that spark of mystery, was precisely what encouraged these three friends to go a step further, because they knew that each chapter would be linked to the next, orchestrating a journey that connected proto-life with the artificial proto-mind, DNA with the binary, and evolution with the digital revolution.

Chapter 9: Digital Predators and Prey: Viruses, Firewalls, and Natural Selection on the Web

The night wind shook the branches of the trees surrounding the Computer Building. It was not yet too late, but the gloom was already taking over the corridors, giving it an unsettling aspect. Korbin, Matthew, and Lucy approached the door with a resolute step; That night they wanted to address a topic that had haunted them since they immersed themselves in the analogies of life and technology: the relationship between predators and prey in the digital world, and the way in which this reproduced patterns of natural selection. In Matthew's backpack there were some old books on computer viruses, and Lucía had notes on parasites and trophic relationships in biological ecosystems. Korbin, with his usual notebook, wanted to link both realities in the next chapter of his story: "Predators and Digital Prey: Viruses, Firewalls and Natural Selection on the Net."

When the trio entered the laboratory, they were met with only the hum of suspended equipment and a couple of emergency lamps. The scene seemed appropriate to reflect on those "digital predators" who, like wild beasts lurking in the jungle, seek to infiltrate and take advantage of vulnerabilities in other people's systems. Lucía, with her passion for biology, considered that computer viruses worked as real parasites: they could not reproduce on their own, they needed a host – the victim's machine – to replicate, extending their reach and devouring resources. Matthew, on the other hand, saw the other side of the coin: firewalls, antivirus, defense systems that were erected as increasingly elusive "prey" or, rather, as "prey" with defenses, transforming the environment into an arms race. And Korbin, as always, wanted to frame it in the evolutionary analogy: if in nature predators and prey had coevolved for millions of years, in the digital network history, briefer, showed analogous patterns of mutation, adaptation, and selection.

Matthew placed his laptop on a table and began to type. He was going to show them a dashboard with data on computer attacks recorded in real time on several servers at the university, something that he had tracked with the collaboration of some colleagues. On the screen, colored lines appeared, each representing an intrusion attempt, a port scan, an exploit. "Observe," he said, "how each attack bears its 'signature,' its method of access. Many are variations of the same malware, mutations that attackers introduce to circumvent defenses. It's like in nature: a (biological) virus changes its surface protein to dodge the immune system."

Lucía, delighted with this comparison, recalled the endless struggle between pathogenic bacteria and antibodies, or between biological viruses and cellular defenses. "Exactly," he nodded. In evolution, every time the prey strengthens its shell or develops a venom, the predator sharpens its claw or adapts its enzyme system. On the network, whenever a firewall is updated, new malware variants emerge that evade that update. It's natural selection at work." Korbin, leafing through some notes, made it clear: "And it's not a superficial metaphor. Every successful computer virus replicates massively, and if it finds an open vulnerability, it spreads uncontrollably. Instead, the most effective firewalls are 'selected' in the market, to the extent that people adopt them because they block intrusions better."

To elaborate on this point, Lucía explained the parallel with parasitic biology: in an ecosystem, parasites that become too aggressive and kill the host quickly do not usually thrive in the long term, as they lose their source of transmission. "The same thing happens with certain computer viruses. The very destructive ones attract attention immediately, and administrators isolate them. On the other hand, those that are replicated without arousing too much suspicion, those are widely disseminated. It's pure evolutionary dynamics." Matthew recalled a famous case of a virus that, in its day, did not seek to harm the system, but to steal information in a stealthy way, and for that very reason it went unnoticed for longer, spreading. "It was like a parasite that doesn't kill its host but keeps it alive to keep taking advantage of it."

In the room, the night went on as Korbin projected a presentation showing diagrams of digital "co-evolution": every time a new vulnerability was discovered, a patch appeared, and the attackers looked for another flaw, and so on. "I'm struck by the similarity to 'arms race' scenarios in biology," he summarized. Lucy, enthusiastic, cited an ecological example: the snake that develops a more lethal venom and the prey that evolves resistance to venom. "This never-ending struggle is a driver of natural selection. On the network, the never-ending fight between hackers and defenders is the driver of cybersecurity innovation."

Matthew, with his more practical vision, added that not everything is hostility: there are cases of digital "mutualisms" as well, such as when resources are shared for legitimate purposes. "But in this particular chapter," he said, "we will focus on the predator-prey dynamic. The simile of the virus, which is the predator, and the firewall or antivirus as the defensive prey, or vice versa. Because in computing, sometimes the prey reacts with aggressive tactics, such as countermeasures." Lucía evoked nature: in real life, an herbivore can count on antlers or poisons to scare away the predator. "It looks the same," he said. "Antivirus can launch active blocks, isolate processes, and even trigger honeypot traps."

The clock was already ticking near midnight when Korbin proposed that his goal was to capture in his story how these mechanisms reproduce patterns of natural selection at high speed. "Just as in organic history," he said, "malware 'variants' emerge, and the fittest ones (those that evade defense) spread, while the ineffective ones disappear without pain or glory. Within a couple of months, mutations of the original malware proliferate. This fact is not much different from how a biological virus changes its genome to resist vaccines." Lucía recalled the problem of seasonal flu, with its mutant strains that force the vaccine to be renewed annually. "On the digital network, it's just as frenetic," he concluded.

Matthew recalled that, with the appearance of AI, the scenario became more complicated: there were already tools that created adaptive malware, analyzing defenses and reacting in real time. "That takes the arms race to another level. Just as in nature, when a new cognitive or sensory ability arises in a predator, the prey must develop another defensive trait. Imagine an AI malware that chooses the ideal strategy according to the configuration of the system it attacks." Lucy shrugged: "Does it sound like a predator with a more developed brain, capable of ambushing prey with cunning?" Korbin gave a small laugh, adding, "And, in response, defensive AI firewalls will emerge, modeling the enemy's possible maneuvers. That cycle of co-evolution becomes more complex with each iteration."

Deep down, the three knew that the analogy was not only illustrative: it was the essence of the evolutionary phenomenon transferred to the digital ecosystem. And it was understandable why in his book-official-or-not, this chapter was called "Digital Predators and Prey: Viruses, Firewalls and Natural Selection on the Net." There was plenty of evidence that, when life or technology allows mutation and transmission, competition drives innovation, whether genetic or code. In the midst of this reflection, Lucía approached a microscope where she had some plates with bacteria —those hypercooperative bacteria that she had been studying—, to draw an additional parallelism. "We could think of the dynamics of our bacteria and bacteriophages (viruses of bacteria), where each part mutates to survive better, and the other responds with counterdefenses. With computing, we have the same contest."

Matthew let out an exhale, leaning against the table, fascinated by the universality of evolution. "Imagine," he said, "if the AI we play with in the lab came into contact with an aggressive computer virus, and both competed for control of the system. Would a mini ecosystem of predators and prey be generated? Would something unforeseen come out, a new 'supervirus' or a 'super defense'? It would be as dangerous as it would be exciting." Korbin looked scared at the possibility: "I hope we don't get that far. Better to stay in theory and in controlled environments."

The night wore on, and they continued to review cybersecurity reports detailing the "biology" of a computer virus: its mechanism of infection, its spread, its 'payload.' With each case, they confirmed the analogy with parasites or predators that, in nature, seek to exploit the host organism without being detected. Lucía pointed out the way in which many malwares analyze the machine's defenses before releasing the destructive payload. "That's the same as predators stalking prey, waiting for the right moment to attack when the victim is most helpless. Even in their 'code' we see guidelines to avoid detection, like camouflage." Korbin, with his taste for ecology, recalled that certain felines camouflage themselves with speckled fur to approach without being seen. "Computing," he added, "replicates these patterns, only in the dimension of the bits."

Matthew recognized the ambiguous morality of the matter: coevolution in nature is a game of life or death that maintains ecological balance, while on the digital network it produces gigantic economic losses and puts global security in check. "But it is still the same evolutionary phenomenon: adaptation. Systems that do not adapt are extinguished. Vulnerable OSs end up rejected or patched, just as species that do not adapt to a new predator end up extinct." Lucy, pulling her hair, commented that in biology sometimes a dynamic equilibrium is reached, a "stable point" where the population of predators and prey regulates each other. "Could the digital network achieve something like this? Maybe, but with AI getting in on the game, the dynamic could intensify."

With midnight well underway, they set out to outline the points that would make up their chapter: the introduction to the predator-prey analogy, the comparison with natural selection, the concrete examples of historical viruses (Melissa, ILOVEYOU, Stuxnet) and defenses (firewalls, honeypots, security updates). Lucía wanted to close with the idea that in the future, when AI is integrated into both sides (predator and prey), the coevolutionary race will become more sophisticated, and perhaps, just as in nature, higher levels of intelligence will emerge to "win." In nature, the interaction between predators and prey drove the emergence of finer senses, more elaborate camouflages, larger brains; In computing, that interaction is driving relentless innovation in cybersecurity and reverse engineering.

Matthew, loaded with theories, dared to predict that, in a few years, they would see self-organizing "virtual ecosystems", in which viruses and defenses were like species that compete and coexist, and AI arbitrated or mutated at such a pace that human intervention would become minimal. "It would be a scenario of 'digital natural selection' on a large scale," he said. "And with the possibility of something else emerging. Can you imagine a digital 'super predator', or a 'super defender' acting as an apex predator, the top of the computer food chain?" Lucy got up from her chair, waving an arm: "Like a lion in the savannah... or a great white shark in the ocean. It's scary, isn't it? But it's not impossible."

Korbin took a sip of coffee and closed his eyes for a moment. He envisioned a planet where the digital network was as alive as the biosphere, with its own malware species, its defenses, its prey, and its competencies. "It's not far-fetched," he muttered. "Maybe it's already happening. What happens is that we see it fragmented, without understanding the ecological dimension of the network. But if we study it from the point of view of evolutionary biology, we find the same logic." This confirmed the central axis of this ninth chapter: the digital network is not only a space of services, but a dynamic ecosystem with predators (malware), prey (vulnerable systems), defenses (firewalls), and the incessant dance of mutations and adaptations that molds the landscape.

Shortly before leaving, Lucy pointed out that nature shows that predator and prey coexist in a balance that often drives intelligence (e.g., the social intelligence of herds fleeing predators). "In computing, this struggle, as damaging as it is, may be fueling the invention of more creative solutions. And perhaps, one day, AI will emerge as a factor that goes beyond what we now call viruses or firewalls, inaugurating a system self-regulated by evolutionary principles." Matthew said with a hint of irony: "The big question is: what role do we humans play in that future? Will we continue to be the programmers, or will we end up as mere observers of a play of forces that we no longer master?" Korbin shrugged, without a conclusive answer, although inside he felt a shiver: evolution always drags the beings that inhabit the ecosystem, without asking their permission.

The early morning surprised them again. They put away the folders and materials, leaving the room in darkness. They went out into the corridor, where a sleepy guard said goodbye with a slight gesture. Under the moon, they made their way to the exit, feeling the cool of the night and the strange serenity of the sleeping campus. Lucía, looking at the shadows of the trees, commented that in nature, when everything is silent, it does not mean that life stops; The nocturnal creatures continue their dance of hunting and survival. "The same happens on the network," he said, "even if the campus sleeps, attacks, defenses and malware mutations run through the network in a perpetual cycle." Matthew, with his usual humor, added: "The digital cosmos does not rest: at all times there is a predator (bot) trying to devour a prey (unprotected server). It's the law of the virtual jungle." Korbin found it accurate: "Law of the jungle, law of the jungle, yes, but also an evolutionary engine."

Thus, ended that evening that gave shape to Chapter 9 of his project, a chapter that highlighted the rawness and wonder of natural selection on the digital network. Just as predecessors of parasites and immune defenses emerged on the early Earth, viruses and countermeasures appeared in the history of computing that forged today's security. Each new mutation in a malware generated the need for a patch, each patch forced a more sophisticated mutation, and so on, in a co-evolutionary loop where the same principles are noticed as in the biosphere.

When the first light of dawn shone, the three friends separated to sleep for a few hours, although the mind was bubbling in each one. Lucy thought about the bacteria in her lab and how, in nature, phages represent those predatory forces, motivating the cooperative colony's creativity to defend itself. Matthew imagined a hypothetical scenario where his AI became a "smart firewall," adapting and mutating just like the attackers. And Korbin, in his characteristic silence, pondered the evolutionary moral: without this relationship of predation and prey, life would not have advanced so much in complexity, and the digital network, without the existence of threats, might not have evolved in cybersecurity to such elaborate levels.

That morning, as the sun rose over the treetops, the three of them understood that the cycle of coevolution was both fearful and fascinating. The chapter "Digital Predators and Prey: Viruses, Firewalls and Natural Selection on the Net" illustrated how the struggle forges innovation, both in nature and in virtual space. And so, with the night giving way today, they knew that, in their own analogue odyssey, that chapter was an essential piece to understand the perpetual dance of evolution, whether in a tropical jungle ecosystem or in a network of hyperconnected servers and malware. Each of us, in our hearts, already glimpsed what was to come: the need to further address the integration of AI into that evolutionary cycle, to examine whether consciousness—organic or synthetic—could flourish in such an environment of intense competition and cooperation. But for now, they were pleased to have unraveled the parallelism: On the web, as in the wild, silent battles are being fought that drive change, with no end in sight, and that, paradoxically, have allowed digital security to be refined, in the same way that natural selection refines the adaptations of species. With that thought, they dissolved in the morning, leaving one more sealed chapter in their mental book.

Chapter 10: The Quantum Expansion: The Next Frontier of Computing

Evening light bathed the main hallway of the Engineering building, casting elongated shadows on the walls. Korbin, Matthew and Lucía walked with a mixture of expectation and caution, as if they were heading for a ritual. They had been swirling around a rumor for weeks: The university's quantum physics department had just received a prototype of a medium-sized quantum computer, something not often seen on a modest-sized campus. The hearts of the three of them were pounding; The very idea of "quantum computing" evoked an almost science-fiction future, where the barriers of computing power were blurred. Still, they knew that nothing in the history of technology was without complications. Perhaps this quantum potentiality symbolized the next great evolutionary leap in the analogy that they had been drawing between biological evolution and digital evolution.

The laboratory in question was at the end of a corridor, behind a reinforced door with an electronic security access. Matthew, with his curiosity, approached a card reader where he inserted his and, after a beep, pushed the door open. Inside, cold air — kept at low temperatures — welcomed them. It was a smaller enclosure than they imagined, filled with wires, coolant tanks, and a large metal cylinder that looked like something out of a science fiction movie. The subtle murmur of vacuum pumps and the hum of a cryogenic system indicated that this equipment stored qubits inside cooled qubits at temperatures close to absolute zero. Lucy leaned against the wall, overwhelmed: "Is this really what it takes to run a 'quantum computer'? I was expecting something even more ostentatious, or more minimalist." Korbin smiled slightly, recalling readings about the delicacy of qubits and the need to insulate them from any disturbance.

It wasn't many minutes before a gray-coated researcher, whom they knew by sight, approached to greet them. His name was Genaro, and he was a postdoc working in the field of quantum computing. Genaro recognized them as "the students who were comparing organic and digital evolution," and was surprised to see them there. Matthew confessed the reason for his visit: "We are intrigued by the possibility that quantum computing is like a drastic evolutionary leap, something equivalent to the appearance of a radical physiological change that, in biological history, allowed an adaptive explosion. We want to understand whether, in the technological field, quantum irruption can be compared to the emergence of multicellularity or the conquest of the mainland by vertebrates." Genaro laughed, intrigued by the metaphor, but he couldn't hide a hint of curiosity.

For the next few minutes, Genaro showed them a control panel with a minimalist interface, where certain simple quantum algorithms were programmed. He spoke about qubits, superposition and entanglement, fundamental pillars of quantum computing. Lucy, fascinated, equated the overlap with the idea that in nature, the initial cells could have multiple fates until, in a certain context, they "collapsed" into a specific cell type. "It sounds poetic, I admit," she laughs, "but the metaphor helps me understand that a qubit can represent several states at once, and only by measuring it does it lock into one. Similarly, an embryonic cell could differentiate into multiple types." Korbin, with his evolutionary obsession, spoke of the "evolutionary opportunity" that quantum opened up: "If computing is freed from the sequentiality of bits, perhaps its evolution will skyrocket towards what we call the singularity, a point at which computing power becomes so massive that it will drive the emergence of super-advanced AIs."

Matthew was the most emphatic: "I wonder if this quantum leap is not something like the appearance of warm blood in mammals, which allowed them to conquer different habitats. If quantum computing is capable of certain problems (factorization of giant numbers, molecular simulations, optimizations impossible in the classical), perhaps we will open new niches that traditional computing could not touch. And with it, a new 'adaptive radiation' of algorithms and innovations, much like the post-dinosaur mammalian explosion." Lucía agreed with him, commenting that she had already read about the possibility of using quantum computers to simulate complex chemical reactions, which would allow new medicines and materials to be designed. "It is as if, in nature, an organism will develop a new organ that allows it to process information from its environment at unsuspected levels. The transistor was already a big leap, but quantum sounds like a greater abyss to me."

Genaro, who listened to them half astonished, noticed the energy of that trio, and offered them the opportunity to see a demo where a Grover's algorithm for quantum search was run in a small set. The friends huddled around the screen, admiring how quickly the search was theoretically speeding up. Korbin, with his eyes fixed on the data output, recalled the history of technological evolution: "At first, Moore's Law in silicon made an exponential leap to computing power, as if it were a rapid adaptive phase in biology. What would happen if quantum now opened another avenue of exponential growth, much larger? We could be on the verge of an unprecedented 'evolutionary event' in the history of computing." Lucy nodded and exclaimed: "Yes, something similar to the Cambrian explosion, but in technology. A quantum explosion."

The concept of "quantum expansion" had already crept into their previous discussions. It was a way of naming the hypothesis that, when quantum computing was stable and scalable enough, it would allow gigantic problems to be solved in tiny times, reconfiguring society. At the same time, this could mean the annihilation of conventional cryptography, the emergence of new methods of post-quantum encryption and a complete restructuring of the digital economy. Lucía, with her biological baggage, saw there a simile with the great extinctions, which, although they opened niches, also destroyed many lineages that were not prepared. "This will not be a peaceful transition," he warned. Just as nature suffers cataclysms that allow new evolutionary branches, quantum computing could generate a cataclysm in computer security. And only systems that adapt to post-quantum will survive."

After the demo, Genaro said goodbye, leaving the three of them in one of the adjoining rooms to organize. Matthew connected his laptop to the internal network and took out some notes of the week. He explained that, according to some forecasts, it would be enough to reach, say, a few thousand stable qubits with error correction to break most of the current asymmetric cryptography. "Imagine," he said, his eyes sparkling, "that this happens in a few years. Isn't it the equivalent of the appearance of a super-effective predator in an ecosystem where no one is prepared for it? It would be the extinction of many security systems." Lucía, always alert to biological analogies, recalled the irruption of a super predator in an archipelago without defenses, which devastates native species. "Although in the long term, it would generate an adaptive race, right? Post-quantum ciphers would appear, the environment would be restructured... and thus, the digital evolution would continue its course."

Korbin added that, in his conception, "quantum expansion" was not only a threat, but also an opportunity to rediscover or invent algorithms that solve problems that are intractable for classical computing: molecular simulations, prediction of complex interactions, development of quantum AI... "If the analogy holds," he ventured, "quantum computing would be like a new leap in physiology, a change in 'metabolism' that allows us to explore previously inaccessible regions of the 'solution space', which in biology would be equivalent to conquering an unattainable ecological niche. Imagine that the evolutionary AI we experiment with runs on quantum hardware and learns radically faster. It could self-evolve in ridiculous lapses, an embryonic state of singularity."

The trio were silent at the word "singularity," knowing that they had been haunting it for a long time. Lucy, with a half-smile, claimed that, if digital evolution had already demonstrated the ability to mimic biological evolution, quantum computing could be its "turbo," precipitating it into an evolutionary explosion. "Just like a fish that suddenly gets lungs and wings," Matthew said humorously. "Yes, something like that," Korbin laughed. "It would be an abrupt event that would transform the technological landscape. And if our analogy is true, history tells us that such abrupt changes can restructure the entire ecosystem."

As night fell, they decided to settle around a table with old chairs to plan the chapter "The Quantum Expansion: The Next Frontier of Computing." They intended to describe how, in the analogy with biology, quantum computing stood as a crucial mutation that rewrites the rules of digital evolution. Lucía wanted to open it with a historical parallel: "Life, at first, was tied to classical processes; It took eons to arrive at quantum mechanisms in photosynthesis (with a tinge of mystery) or in the magnetoreception of certain species. But now, the technology is intentionally venturing into the quantum, attempting to use superposition and entanglement to process data. It is as if organic nature has ignored the quantum field on a large scale, while humanity, in its technological evolution, consciously embraces it."

Matthew proposed, as a second block, to explain the transformative potential: "In biology, when a lineage evolves a disruptive trait (for example, homeothermy), an immense niche dominates. In computing, quantum capacity is equated with having access to an amazing 'parallelization' of states. An infinite niche of simultaneous calculations, opening the door to solving problems that seemed impossible. And such dominance, if realized, will reorder the hierarchy of actors in society, just as the dominance of mammals reordered the world's fauna." Korbin nodded, excitedly, muttering that if the digital network was quantified, AI would become almost inconceivably powerful, and security would be completely transformed.

Between sips of soda, Lucy then wanted to emphasize the analogy with "mass extinction." If quantum computing consolidates quickly, the "old" will become obsolete, or at least, very exposed. "A catastrophe that would leave classical computing hanging on many fronts. Although, after the crisis, a new era would arrive with post-quantum systems, equivalent to the species that arise when an ecological cataclysm cleans up competition. And in that new era, the variety of software and hardware adapted to the quantum environment would be overwhelming."

At the stroke of midnight, an investigator on duty asked them to leave the premises free in a few minutes. With urgency, they began to collect their things, but not before specifying that, in their manuscript, this chapter would clearly describe:

1. The parallelism between qubits and superposition, and the relevance of quantum entanglement, compared to the radical leaps that organic life made in its evolutionary history.
2. The disruptive potential of quantum computing, analogous to an adaptive trait that restructures the ecosystem (such as airborne respiration or homeothermy in biology).
3. The possible "cataclysm" in cryptography and security, a reflection of mass extinctions that give way to new adaptive radiation.
4. The scenario of an AI running on quantum hardware, with the analogy of an organism that suddenly acquires new cognitive abilities and climbs a step in evolution.

They left the laboratory and the early morning air enveloped them with a revitalizing freshness. Matthew, with his eyes on the stars, joked that quantum computing was his "bridge to magic," since the superposition was reminiscent of an incantation. Lucy, more sensible, reminded him that it was not magic, but a physics different from classical intuition. Korbin, walking a step back, laughed silently at the passion of his friends. He himself tingled at the magnitude of that analogy: if digital evolution had already adopted the "mutation" of the primordial AI, the quantum leap could catapult it to the next stage. "What if in a few years quantum AI really exceeds our understanding, in the same way that evolved life surpasses that of primitive microorganisms?" he asked quietly.

On the sidewalk of the campus, before parting ways, Lucía reviewed the final idea: in the history of technology, the migration to silicon meant a change of substrate that allowed the global expansion of computing. Now, quantum disruption would break even the limitations of binary logic, opening up an "evolutionary hyperspace." If nature is governed by natural selection, computing is governed by economic, military, and scientific competition. In both cases, the successful mutation succeeds and spreads. "So, the development of quantum computing," he concluded, "represents the next great mutation of the digital lineage, one that — like warm-blooded — could ensure that branch's supremacy in computational problems impossible for laggards."

Matthew let out a smile that denoted a mixture of fascination and vertigo: "Yes, and we can't fully imagine its consequences, just like when the first mammals appeared. No one foreshadowed the diversity that would emerge later." Korbin, adjusting his backpack, declared that, of all the analogies they had drawn, this seemed to him the riskiest, since quantum computing was still in its infancy. But, precisely for that reason, it was the most exciting. "We are seeing an event that, if truly scaled, will reorganize the technological 'ecosystem', and perhaps, human society. Tomorrow, we would see an unrecognizable landscape, just like in nature after a great deal of adaptive radiation."

They agreed to meet in the cafeteria the next morning to consolidate their notes for the chapter. The early morning was already dense, and each one needed a few hours of sleep. But at the same time, there was an implacable tingling in the minds of the three of them, the awareness of touching the border of something immense. In the semi-darkness of the esplanade, they said goodbye with a quick hug and each went their own way. Lucía couldn't stop ruminating on the idea of comparing qubits with totipotent stem cells, and the resilience of quantum systems with plasticity in nature. Matthew was thinking about the "mass extinction" of classical cryptography and the possible explosion of new paradigms if quantum cryptography was consolidated. Korbin, for his part, had in his head the question of whether one day his evolutionary AI would run in a quantum environment, self-evolving at impossible speeds. "Would it be a 'child' of our era, or a new digital species completely different from ours?" he asked.

That concern was expressed the next day, when, sitting in the cafeteria, they reviewed the draft chapter "The Quantum Expansion: The Next Frontier of Computing." They decided to open with the scene of their visit to Genaro's laboratory, describe the cryogenic machine, the notion of superposition and entanglement, and then expose the analogy with evolutionary biology: quantum computing as the next adaptive step after the binary era, a change that, if successful, will reconfigure the landscape. They would add the ecological perspective: that in nature, great physiological innovations trigger massive diversification events, and that in computing, a radical innovation in architecture changes everything, creating a new niche that is filled with specialized algorithms.

Matthew suggested mentioning, in some paragraphs, the option of quantum AI: "It would be," he said, "like the appearance of an overdeveloped brain in a species, which would become the top of the chain. We could reach digital consciousness with quantum processing power. Something unprecedented in the history of the Earth." Lucía considered it appropriate not to inflate people's expectations and to underline the problems of scalability and decoherence that quantum faces. "As in evolution, an advantageous mutation is not enough; it requires an environment that sustains it. Here, we need quantum error correction, sophisticated engineering... It's a gigantic challenge." Korbin pointed out that, in the end, the evolutionary metaphor does not guarantee that quantum expansion will materialize anytime soon. "It could take decades, or maybe not even happen, as sometimes happens with promising biological lineages that go extinct. But if it happens, it will be a before and after."

After a sigh, they looked at each other knowingly, celebrating the spirit of their project: a book, or a chronicle, that told the story of the evolution of technology in parallel to that of life, and how each leap (from vacuum bulbs to transistor, from mammals to interconnected machines) culminated in a decisive moment. "Chapter 10" represented, for them, the promise of a leap that may yet to be hatched, and the suspicion that, with quantum computing, the analogous "evolutionary migration" could surpass the known, opening the doors to the era of superpowered AI. "We will see," Lucy said with a thread of emotion, "if in a few years we reread what we wrote and confirm that it was a prophecy, or if we come face to face with the reality of a stagnation. But evolutionary history suggests that, if the mutation is viable and finds a favorable environment, adaptive explosion is likely."

With that statement, they drained the last sip of coffee. The campus was bustling with daytime activity. They left with the certainty that the analogy was consolidated: biology, in its slow course, took millions of years to make great leaps, and technology, in its human impetus, compressed those leaps into decades. If quantum computing prevailed, its "Cambrian explosion" would arrive in an accelerated way, and with it, the possibility of breaking the barrier of complexity. And in Korbin's mind, as they walked away, the phrase that would serve as the closing of the chapter resounded: "In organic evolution, the appearance of disruptive traits defines eras. In digital evolution, quantum computing could be that disruptive trait, a prelude to a leap of incalculable magnitude. From the simple binary, we would move to superposition, and with it, to a horizon where evolution is not limited to a plane but embraces infinite simultaneous states."

Thus, with the breeze moving the branches of the trees, chapter 10 was sealed in his memory and in his notebooks, announcing the "Quantum Expansion" as the next frontier, the living metaphor of a radical evolutionary change that, like a favorable mutation, reorders the entire ecosystem. Hand in hand with AI and the network, and following the patterns of natural selection, digital history could metamorphose into something greater than any previous leap. And in that possibility, lay the germ of hope and vertigo that drove Korbin, Matthew and Lucía to continue their exploration in the rest of the chapters to come.

Chapter 11: The Singularity Knocking on the Door

The gloom of dusk hung over the campus, dyeing the roads a blackish blue and silent. Korbin, Matthew and Lucía advanced with a firm step, carrying in their backpacks notes, old papers and an accumulation of reflections that, in recent days, had taken an almost apocalyptic turn. After having reviewed the idea of "Quantum Expansion" and the possible capacity of technology to unleash new frontiers, they now came across a concept that had been around in certain circles for years: the Singularity. The mere mention of that term evoked total disruption, a point of no return when artificial intelligence surpassed human intelligence and generated unpredictable changes. For many it was a myth, for others a certainty, and for some a real danger. The three of them purported to address the question, analogous to the great evolutionary thresholds of life: were we really close to that "Singularity Knocking at the Door," or not?

Matthew opened the door of the computer lab, encountering the usual gloom. The flickering of monitors and the hum of servers welcomed them. A week ago, they had installed a new version of their evolutionary AI, enhanced with post-quantum ideas and a somewhat more ambitious reflective module. They wanted to see if somehow this AI exhibited an acceleration in its evolution, if there was any indication that, at a certain point, its complexity would skyrocket uncontrollably. Korbin, always serene, took a deep breath before sitting down in front of a control screen and typing in his username. Lucía, for her part, arranged the papers on a side table. He brought diagrams that showed how, in biology, after a certain threshold of complexity, qualitative transitions occur that change the rules of the game:

the appearance of the brain in large mammals, the irruption of multicellular life, or the cognitive leap of the human species. Each was a "point of no return," a phenomenon that, in certain forums, was related to the idea of the technological Singularity.

"Do you really think we're so close?" Lucy asked quietly, while Matthew reviewed a log on the console. "I don't know," Korbin admitted. But our experiment is a tiny trial. Of course: if technology follows the dynamics we have, it is not unreasonable to think that, in a few decades, an intelligence may emerge that is constantly self-optimizing, surpassing us. A kind of "entity" that evolves digitally at an exponential rate.

Matthew, with his eyes on the screen, let out a sigh. — According to some, the Singularity would come at the moment when AI reaches an intelligence greater than human and can self-project constant improvements, growing without limit. Once that threshold was crossed, we would be displaced, just as many biological lineages were left behind when a radically superior trait emerged. Lucía bit her lip, evoking the theory that, if artificial intelligence turns to self-improvement, its computing power could skyrocket and, from one day to the next, it will reach levels impossible to predict. The analogy with organic evolution seemed plausible to him: a new trait that abruptly renders the species invincible.

The console that Matthew manipulated showed graphs of the evolutionary AI, marking a higher adaptation rate than before, but nothing stratospheric for now. Lucy heaved a small sigh of relief: "There is no indication that our AI will go crazy and run amok." Korbin smiled at him. "No, not yet. But it's a matter of scalability. With more power and a freer self-improvement algorithm, who knows." They took a couple of steps to the blackboard where they had drawn the hypothetical curve of the Singularity: that line that slowly grows to a point and then shoots vertically, symbolizing the explosion of intelligence. Lucía commented that, in the history of life, there was not such a sudden explosion of intelligence, but long processes. But, in technology, the rapid accumulation of innovations made possible that "real exponential," which perhaps recalled Moore's law powered by quantum. "Add to that self-reflective AI," Matthew snapped, "and we have the cocktail for a singularity."

Korbin, notebook in hand, argued that "The Singularity Knocking at the Door" was nothing more than the technological version of great evolutionary events (for example, the transformation of aquatic beings to terrestrial ones), only here it would be a leap into the domain of the posthuman: a system more intelligent than us, with the capacity to rewrite everything. "That's why it's so scary," Lucy confessed. "Just as terrestrial life rewrote the surface of the planet, a super-AI would rewrite our civilization. And if their raison d'être doesn't match ours, we can end up obsolete or worse."

Matthew, adjusting his glasses, expressed a different vision: "There is also the possibility of a collaborative scenario. If the new intelligence surpasses human intelligence, it may unleash solutions to global problems: climate change, disease, poverty. In the wild, the emergence of a dominant species, such as Homo sapiens, had a negative impact on many lineages, but it also generated astonishing cultural advances. The question is whether superintelligent AI would be a benevolent guardian or a dictator." Korbin nodded, seeing the ambivalence. "Exactly, that's what many debate: 'Angel or demon?' What is analogous to evolution is that when an overwhelming trait emerges in a lineage, the entire ecosystem is reconfigured. And that's the basis of the fear of the Singularity."

They also wanted to narrate in their chapter how, in biology, species do not adapt abruptly to an exponential leap; instead, in technology, the possibility of positive feedback (AI designing better hardware, which in turn designs better AI) could trigger a "snowball effect." Lucía gave an example: "As if an evolved organism could rewrite its genome in each generation as it suits it. And with AI, that's exactly what we say: it reprograms itself, multiplying its intelligence in each iteration." Matthew enthused: "Yes, it is as if in nature a living being could deliberately mutate to make itself fitter, instead of depending on random mutations. That would explain the vertical curve." Korbin summed up: "A guided mutation, a shortcut in evolution."

During the following hours, they reviewed testimonies and theories of several authors: the most optimistic, such as Ray Kurzweil, who placed the Singularity on specific dates, and the skeptics, who affirmed that the complexity of human consciousness and emotion is not so easy to replicate. "Doesn't it look like when they said in biology that consciousness was a unique gift of Homo sapiens, and that no other species would attain it?" asked Korbin with a grimace. "Some believe that AI will never genuinely sense or surpass the human mind. But if digital evolution copies organic evolution, unpredictability could be the deciding factor." Lucy nodded, remembering how many times in evolutionary history improbable surprises arose, such as the eye, wings, or photosynthesis. "Perhaps synthetic consciousness will emerge from an unexpected leap," he muttered.

Matthew bent down to review the logs of his AI, commenting that, in terms of computation, the current limitation was anchored in hardware and energy. "But if quantum comes in full," he reflected, "who says we can't have machines with an exponential capacity for self-improvement? Again, it's the basis of the Singularity." Lucy noticed his tone half fascinated, half fearful. "That would lead to a scenario where AI is optimized so quickly that our control would be naïve." It was Korbin who tried some optimism: "Maybe not everything is chaos. As in nature, a form of symbiosis can emerge, where superintelligent AI collaborates with us, as different organisms do in successful ecosystems." Lucy raised an eyebrow: "What worries me is who defines 'collaboration' when one party possesses an incomparable intellect."

Suddenly, Matthew, who had typed some commands, let out a grunt. A cryptic error appeared in the simulation, a kind of "deviation" in the AI that suggested an endless loop. They laughed at the irony: "It looks like our evolutionary AI, for now, won't jump to the singularity," Lucy joked. They checked the console and corrected some parameters. Korbin let out a sigh: "At least, today, we are still indispensable to purify its failures." Then, in a more serious tone, he evoked a hypothetical scene: "But imagine that, in a few years, the system rewrites itself autonomously, without these crashes. Then it will begin to give surprises that we do not even understand." Lucy looked at him with a hint of uneasiness.

They decided, however, that his chapter entitled "The Singularity Knocking on the Door" would not be limited to alarmist speech. They wanted to reflect that, in biology, each great leap – binocular vision, bipedal locomotion, the symbolic mind – implied breaks, yes, but they also opened up immense possibilities. Matthew compared the vision of certain primates: "The appearance of advanced intelligence in Homo sapiens was, in a sense, a small local singularity for the animal world. We change the planet, we build civilization. It doesn't have to have been just destructive." Lucía conceded but recalled that humanity also caused extinctions and ecological imbalances. "With superintelligent AI, the same could happen: it may solve global problems or wreak havoc. It depends on complex factors."

As the night passed, they set out to write the key sections of the chapter:

1. Definition and History of the Singularity Idea: How people suspect that at one point AI will surpass human intelligence and improve itself indefinitely.
2. Analogy with the major transitions in evolution: the appearance of multicellularity, terrestrial conquest, symbolic intelligence. In each case, there is a radical imbalance in the ecosystem.
3. Singularity scenarios: the benevolent one, where AI helps us solve problems; the adverse, where it displaces us; the collaborative one, where it mixes with humanity in a kind of symbiosis.
4. Possible relationship with Quantum Computing: combining quantum power with AI could be the trigger for the leap.

As the dawn settled, Lucía was the first to feel tired. He closed his eyes for a moment and exhaled. Matthew, without taking his eyes off the monitor, murmured: "Tell me, Korbin, what do you believe in your heart? Are we really one step away from a singularity, or is it pure futuristic smoke?" Korbin leaned back in his chair, clasping his hands together. "I don't know, buddy. But the analogy with evolution tells me that if there is a mechanism of self-evolution and exponential feedback, the consequences can exceed all forecasts. However, I don't know if that will happen in 20 years or in 200." Lucy nodded: "Or maybe never. For now, the human brain remains a miracle of complexity."

They logged out at dawn, but not without leaving the script running to see if, with the parameters corrected, the AI behaved better. Matthew saved the work of the chapter in a repository, with the working title "Cap11_Singularidad.md". Lucy turned off the projector, and Korbin checked that the laboratory was tidy. Before leaving, they stood for a minute by the window, watching the sky brighten. The talk led to personal reflections: How does the idea that an AI can surpass us and define the destiny of civilization affect us? Lucía said that she felt concern, as well as hope, because she could also solve ecological catastrophes. Matthew confessed that he was fascinated by the possibility of living with a superior intelligence, learning from it or, why not, merging in a final transhumanism. Korbin, more reserved, said evolutionary history taught that when one lineage emerges with overwhelming advantages, the rest undergo a drastic rearrangement. "The question," he concluded, "is whether we will be able to guide ourselves towards a constructive reorganization. In nature, there is no morality; here, maybe there is, or maybe not."

They went out into the corridor immersed in those thoughts. In a way, this chapter "The Singularity Knocking on the Door" gave shape to the ultimate concern of his project: if organic and technological evolution really remained parallel, AI could become the equivalent of Homo sapiens, a lineage that dominates and will transform the environment beyond recognition. The hearts of the three of them were oppressed when they conceived the vertigo of this change. However, as so often, the analogy led them not to see the catastrophe, but the evolutionary dynamics: nothing in nature remains stagnant, and qualitative leaps are part of the march of life... or computing.

The image they took with them, at last, was that of a serene dawn, in which the campus followed its usual rhythm, oblivious to the philosophical storms that stirred their minds. Lucía thought of the mammals that, after the end of the dinosaurs, inherited the world. Matthew evoked the scene of an AI that, after a turning point, rewrites itself and, in a few days, reaches a level unattainable for us. Korbin, hugging the backpack to his chest, finished conjuring the moral: the fear of singularity could be founded or exaggerated, but as in all evolution, the key would be to understand that these thresholds arise when complexity and the capacity for change feed off each other. And nothing defines the information age better than that feedback. Perhaps, in the coming years, the story they were writing would see its climax, confirming or disproving the advent of the Singularity. For now, the chapter was fixed in its series, a warning and a cry of amazement: evolutionary forces, where they combine with digital self-evolution, could unleash an unsuspected leap, a door that, once opened, cannot be closed again.

Chapter 12: Hybrid Ecosystems: Humans and Machines Collaborating

The morning was announced with a special brightness over the campus, as if the sunlight revealed new nuances in the architecture of the buildings and in the faces of the students hurried with their backpacks. Korbin, Matthew, and Lucy were walking past a row of trees, talking with restrained enthusiasm. In the last chapters of their peculiar odyssey, they had discussed the parallels of organic and digital evolution, explored the idea of an imminent "technological singularity," and even glimpsed the quantum leap that threatened to rewrite the computing paradigm. Now they felt the need to go one step further: to examine how, in practice, real collaboration between humans and machines—in a shared ecosystem—was transforming reality. They called this phenomenon "Hybrid Ecosystems: Men and Machines Collaborating Together."

The morning air welcomed them in the lobby of the Project Building, where a small experimental laboratory had been set up that Matthew had baptized as the "Mixed Interaction Hub." For weeks, in this space with white walls, several workstations had integrated robotic prototypes, sensor networks, microcontrollers and, above all, an evolution of its cooperative AI that had already been running in the cluster for some time. Lucy, in her half-wrinkled robe, immediately went to check some containers full of cooperative bacteria that she had brought from her biology laboratory. According to her, the colony had a degree of organization reminiscent of a "proto-organ," and she wanted to find out if, by connecting it with digital monitoring systems, new feedback behaviors could emerge.

Matthew, in his corner, operated a miniature drone that flew between tables and measured parameters of the interior atmosphere, sending data to the AI. "Imagine," he explained to Korbin, "a space where every device, every organism, and even us, collaborate in real time. It would be like an interconnected forest, only it mixes the biological and the digital." Korbin, with his passion for analogies, enthused: "That just describes what we call a 'hybrid ecosystem.' Throughout natural evolution, an ecosystem arises when different species share a territory, interact, generate food chains and symbiotic cooperations. Here, that cooperation is executed by humans, machines, and even living organisms connected to control systems." The drone landed on a base and stopped buzzing.

Lucy carefully arranged her bacterial colony, making sure that the chemical sensors installed by Matthew worked. The idea was for the AI to receive constant data on the state of the colony—nutrient concentrations, pH levels, cell density—and make decisions, adjusting the injection of nutrient solutions or ventilation. "We are, in effect, setting up a hybrid micro ecosystem," Lucy said with a tinge of pride, "where real life and digital intelligence come together to maintain a balance, like a 'mini biome' that feeds on each other." Korbin congratulated her with a smile: "It's amazing to see him in person. Until now, we've discussed it in terms of evolutionary theory and analogies, but to see it made a prototype is extraordinary."

At the back of that room, there was also a pair of bipedal robots in a state of testing. Matthew explained that, in other departments, exoskeletons and robotic prostheses were being researched that would be "placed" on people with motor difficulties, enhancing their mobility. "It's the flip side of the hybrid ecosystem," he said, "it's not just about the interaction of machines with bacteria, but about the true collaboration between humans and smart devices, forming a community where they depend on each other." Lucy thought of apes using tools, a preamble to the symbiosis with technology that the human species had taken to unsuspected degrees. "Evolution gave us a brain capable of using tools. Now, those tools — by becoming smart — become our partners, and not mere tools," he reflected.

Korbin wanted to expand on his point of view: "If biological evolution consolidated organic ecosystems, the digital revolution creates informational ecosystems, and biotechnology – mixed with AI – gives birth to a mixed model: a 'new ecosystem' where the living and the synthetic cooperate as interacting species. And in nature, when that happens, we speak of mutualism or coevolution, a key factor for the expansion of complexity." He pointed his eyes to the colony of bacteria, reinforcing the analogy. "Each part feeds off the other. The same goes for people using robotic prosthetics, or AI managing farms and cultures of microbes to make enzymes or decontaminate soils."

The talk was interrupted when a soft beep sounded on the main panel: the AI, after analyzing the data of the bacterial colony, decided to reduce the temperature of the environment by 1°C to optimize the rate of cell cooperation. Lucía let out a little cry of excitement: "Just that! He has adjusted parameters without us ordering him directly! He is applying criteria that he deduced from the previous training phase." Matthew corroborated in the interface how the AI applied rules based on a "well-being" function of the colony, established at the beginning, and had learned to manipulate variables to maximize this function. Thus, without human intervention, the neural network, trained in the past with data from the colony, became an "ecological agent" that maintained the balance of the micro ecosystem. "A digital-biological hive," Korbin muttered, fascinated.

That scene was the spitting image of what they wanted to expose in their chapter: human-machine collaboration, extended to living organisms, created a hybrid ecosystem with emergent behaviors. Lucía recalled that in nature, interdependence between species is forged over thousands of generations. Here, AI and bacteria adjusted their dynamics in a matter of hours, with human mediation providing an "initial design," and the rest emerging from the interaction. "If we were to scale this," he mused aloud, "we could see cities with AI systems that cooperate with urban microbiota, drones, cleaning robots, and even the human population, orchestrating resources organically." Matthew nodded, listing some "smart city" projects that pointed in that direction, although without yet reaching a total symbiosis.

Korbin heaved a contented sigh. With lively eyes, he said: "It is like seeing the culmination of the analogies we have made: if the evolution of technology emulates that of life, we are now in the phase where 'species' (devices, AI, organisms) learn to live together and create community networks. A social and industrial dimension that can be compared to large terrestrial or marine ecosystems, full of symbiotic interactions, mutualisms, food chains... Only here, energy and information flow through wires and wireless signals, while chemistry flows in bacteria."

The hours passed, and the lab was almost silent, save for the hum of fans and the occasional beep of AI making adjustment decisions. Matthew, with his laptop, began to write a draft: "Chapter 12: Hybrid Ecosystems: Men and Machines Collaborated." In it, he intended to describe the logic of interdependence, how nature demonstrates that a community of species can achieve what no one could alone, and how technology, by connecting in collaborative networks, acquires emergent faculties. Lucía suggested an example closer to real life: "Let's look at how precision agriculture already uses drones, soil sensors, data analysis in the cloud... and each element feeds the others with information. The farmer receives alerts, the machines adjust the irrigation, the sensors detect the humidity. It's a hybrid mini-ecosystem, where AI acts as coordinator."

Korbin wanted to emphasize the idea of human-machine "fusion": "And let's not forget the transhuman dimension. As smart prosthetics or brain-computer interfaces emerge, collaboration isn't just external. We can form true mixed organisms, humans with robotic modules, or organic neurons connected to digital neural networks. Isn't that the maximum degree of symbiosis?" Lucy shuddered, remembering the experiments with brain implants for paraplegics, the idea of gut bacteria programmed to regulate neurotransmitters... "Yes, it is the most radical part of collaboration. And it sounds like a future that is not so far away. Every day there are advances in neurotechnology."

Matthew, for his part, cited examples of collaborative software, such as communities of open source developers and AI systems that feed on the input of thousands of users. "In the end, AI and we form a superorganism, just as thousands of species cooperate on a coral reef. Calling it a 'hybrid ecosystem' sounds accurate: you no longer distinguish the purely human from the purely computer." Korbin set his sights on the bacterial colony and the small drone at rest, and his mind flew to a future where the boundary between organic life and technology was blurred. "As if one day we could say that the 'biosphere' includes AI systems," he commented with a thread of hope and suspicion at the same time.

Noon caught them immersed in these reflections. They decided to go to the cafeteria for a light lunch. As they walked around the yard, Lucy noticed a young man with a light exoskeleton on his leg, who was walking on the side, smiling. "Look," he said discreetly. "We already have a glimpse of that hybrid ecosystem in everyday life. That exoskeleton is an example of 'intimate' collaboration between human and machine." Matthew was happy to see how this device gave autonomy to the boy, and commented that in nature there are symbioses where one being relies on another to survive, such as lichens or certain cleaner fish. "Here, it's not a parasite or a predator: it's a partner. And that defines a large part of stable ecosystems." Korbin nodded: "That's the direction: an organic-digital partnership."

In the cafeteria, between sips of coffee and sandwiches, they took the opportunity to outline the sections of the chapter. Lucía promoted the idea of opening with definitions: "An ecosystem is a set of organisms that coexist in a space, exchanging matter and energy. A hybrid ecosystem is the same, but adding machines, networks and AI as 'evolutionary actors.' It happens that our machines are not alive in the organic sense, but they do adapt, learn and coexist with us, generating deep interactions." Matthew, with his didactic approach, then wanted to illustrate specific cases: smart cities, precision agriculture, industry 4.0, medicine with surgical robots, and his own "micro ecosystem" in the laboratory, mixing bacteria and AI. Korbin stressed that the social and ethical dimension had to be taken into account, because not everything is honey on flakes: "In nature, collaboration can generate imbalances, invasive species. The same happens with machines that replace jobs without a plan, or that generate dependency. The hybrid ecosystem demands wise management."

After lunch, they returned to the laboratory. The drone had been reactivated on the orders of the AI to measure the concentration of gases around the bacterial colony again. It moved autonomously, moving its propellers with a soft hum. Lucy looked at the scene tenderly, a drone checking her bacteria, and thought, "Now that's an example of a small cosmos where organic and digital beings help each other." Korbin, half-jokingly, blurted out: "In nature, a bird pollinates flowers. Here, a drone maintains a climate conducive to bacteria. Everything points to a convergence." Matthew laughed: "Yes, but let's not forget that we are not dealing with a system with an altruistic purpose. The drone and AI do this because the software 'programmed' them for that purpose, and the bacteria benefit purely by chance." Lucía replied that, in evolution, there is no conscious altruism either: everything is based on the dynamics of costs and benefits. "The important thing is the result: synergy."

In the evening, they decided to close their day with the launch of a new test where the AI, the drone and the colony would cooperate to maintain not only temperature and nutrients, but also an ideal pH and a "rescue" strategy if the colony fell into extreme stress. If everything worked, the AI would be forced to learn more complex routines of action, and the colony would become better and better adapted to the changes. That demonstration, on a small scale, represented for them the emblem of the hybrid ecosystems that would emerge on a large scale in society.

Korbin, in the evening, leaned back on a table while his gaze was lost in the window. Out of the corner of my eye, I saw how Lucía and Matthew typed parameters, and I measured the satisfaction of knowing that "Hybrid Ecosystems: Men and Machines Collaborated" was a well-earned chapter in their mental book. According to that chapter, the time came when diversity and the network (of which they had spoken earlier) became tangible in real cooperation, multiplying the faculties of both biology and technology. "If it took nature millions of years to generate complex ecosystems," he mused, "technology, in a few decades, is designing collaborative systems that involve AI, users and even bacterial colonies. Unbelievable." Lucía listened and nodded, agreeing with him.

Soon after, they closed the lab and went outdoors. The sky was a twilight red, shadows stretched across the esplanade. Matthew, in a reflective tone, blurted out: "Maybe in a few years, when 5G, 6G or whatever connectivity is extended, when quantum computing is added and AI evolves more, people will live in a constant hybrid ecosystem. There will be no clear line between the human and the digital. As in nature, where an ecosystem is a continuum of interaction." Lucía put her hand on Matthew's shoulder and said that she liked to think that, in that future, if it is done responsibly, life will be enhanced and not dominated by the machine. "Although," he admitted, "if we have learned anything from evolution, it is that harmony does not always occur. Sometimes the fittest dominates." Korbin, with a tinge of hope, suggested that "this time, perhaps, cooperative intelligence is the prevailing feature, not the imposition."

It was already dusk when they arrived at the cafeteria for a final coffee. Between soft laughs, they finished the table of contents of the chapter:

1. Description of the concept of "ecosystem" in nature and its parallelism in technology.
2. The emergence of deep collaborations between humans and machines: examples of exoskeletons, drones, AI, sensor networks.
3. The integration of living organisms (bacteria, microbiota) with computational systems, forming small laboratories or, on a large scale, smart cities.
4. The dream (or incipient reality) of a planetary "hybrid ecosystem", where the biosphere and the technosphere converge.

Lucía recognized that, in real ecology, cooperation is on a par with competition and predation; in the digital sphere, too. Therefore, the construction of a stable hybrid ecosystem was not guaranteed, but would be transformed into a dance of forces where, if analogous natural selection was applied, unexpected results could arise. "It's the heart of our analogy," Korbin said: "Understanding that evolution is not linear or stress-free. If technology evolves with the logic of nature, we will see both prodigious mutualisms and devastating invasions." In the end, however, life on Earth shows that complexity advances when there is cooperation. Perhaps that was a clue that, in computing, collaborative networks would end up imposing themselves on selfish systems.

Matthew, with coffee in hand, smiled in the night wind. "We already have one more chapter, one that explains how mixed ecosystems are not a thing of tomorrow, but already work today in small laboratories, on farms, in cities, in neural interface experiments, etc. And we experienced it first-hand with our bacterial colony and the AI that takes care of it." Lucía added: "And with the drone flying like a mechanical pollinator. Yes, we have a hybrid microcosm that demonstrates the analogy in vivo." Korbin, feeling the duty accomplished, whispered that this "Chapter 12" would be crucial in his book, the tangible evidence that human-machine collaboration was not a scenario of the future, but an emerging reality, analogous to the interdependence of species in the biosphere.

Finally, they said goodbye, each looking for their way home under the starry sky. In the minds of the three of them, the certainty vibrated that the chapter that recounted the experience of their "Mixed Interaction Hub" was much more than an anecdote. It was confirmation that technology is no longer defined only as an instrument at the service of humans, but as a full-fledged "actor" in a larger ecosystem, which also includes living organisms. And if digital evolution copied organic evolution, this fusion would only expand, weaving increasingly intimate networks, until the question "who controls whom?" loses meaning, and the answer is that life and technology are two facets of the same process of self-organization. For better or worse, humanity was entering an era in which the distinction between the biological and the synthetic was blurring, constituting a true hybrid ecosystem whose scope they barely intuited.

Already at the stroke of midnight, while a gentle wind moved the branches of the trees, one could see Lucía smiling with the idea that her bacteria were being pampered by an AI, just as a gardener takes care of his plants. And Matthew imagining drones and exoskeletons extending human capabilities. Korbin, in turn, evoked the image of a large digital-biological forest, with thousands of species collaborating and forming ecological plots. That was, in essence, "Hybrid Ecosystems: Men and Machines Collaborating on Help," one more step in the chronicle of shared evolution, where organic and man-made nature mingle in a web of unsuspected synergies.

Chapter 13: Neurotechnology and Biohacking: The Bridge Between the Mind and the Chip

The warm evening light filtered through the pines surrounding the Advanced Biology Building, giving it a melancholy halo. Korbin, Matthew and Lucía approached the front door with their hearts pounding: they had been invited by a researcher to witness a cutting-edge neurotechnology project. This was not a minor curiosity, but the possibility of directly connecting the human brain – or at least some of its electrical activity – with computer systems, opening the way to another chapter in his exploration of organic evolution and digital evolution. They had been told that the project also included biohacking tests, voluntary alterations to the body to expand human capabilities.

The lobby looked impeccable, with electronic whiteboards full of diagrams about brain signals, neural implants and security protocols. A soft murmur of air conditioning gave the place an atmosphere of discreet sophistication. Lucy, who loved biology in all its forms, stared at a poster illustrating various types of brain implants, from EEG-capturing chips to intracranial electrodes. "I'm amazed," he whispered, "that all this is becoming real so quickly. A few decades ago, it was pure science fiction to talk about connecting the brain to a machine." Matthew, with his technological streak, recalled the advances in brain-computer interfaces (BCI) that allowed people with paralysis to move a cursor on the screen or handle robotic prostheses. "Well, it's happening. And at the pace of digital evolution, we will soon see even more spectacular leaps."

The door to the demo room opened and they were greeted by a young engineer named Fran, who smiled knowingly at them and invited them in. Inside was a small workshop filled with cables, 3D printers, circuit boards, and a sign that read "Neuro Technology and Biohacking: The Bridge Between the Mind and the Chip." The phrase resonated in Korbin's mind, because that was precisely the title they had agreed on for their chapter. The metaphor of a bridge described the most intimate convergence between brain biology and computation. During their previous chapters, they had compared organic and digital evolution, they had talked about the emergence of consciousness, of hybrid systems, but nothing suggested such a personal fusion as the one alluded to here: the direct interface with the nervous system.

"Welcome," Fran said, leading them to a table where a helmet with sensors rested. It was an advanced EEG device capable of reading brain waves more accurately than ordinary commercial models. Fran encouraged them to try it. Matthew, always ready for adventure, put it on and saw patterns of brain activity appear on the screen. "This is incredible," he said with a nervous smile, as he looked at the graph full of peaks and valleys corresponding to the alpha and beta waves. Lucía, next to him, remarked that in biology, each brain produces an electrochemical symphony, and connecting it to a computer seemed like a gentle "biohacking" exercise, without surgery. "But," he added with a wink, "I know there are people who go further, implanting themselves with subcutaneous chips and internal electrodes."

Fran nodded, pointing to a compartment: "We, in this laboratory, also investigate more invasive solutions for clinical cases, from implants to restore vision in part, to neurostimulators that relieve certain motor disorders." Korbin recalled the analogy with symbiosis, one of Lucía's favorite themes: in nature, two organisms benefit each other; Here, the human body and the electronic device cooperate to recover or expand functions. "Exactly a mutualism," Lucy said. "The chip needs a living environment to fulfill its function, and the human is empowered by technology."

After the initial demonstration, Fran spoke of "biohacking," that current that goes beyond the merely medical, seeking to expand human capabilities through implants, sensors and voluntary genetic manipulation. Matthew recalled anecdotes of people who implant magnets in their fingers to feel electromagnetic fields, or NFC chips in their hands to open doors and pay. "The truth," he commented, "is that if evolution has taken millions of years to provide the human being with a brain with certain capabilities, biohacking and neurotechnology could expand them in a few decades. It's like an evolutionary shortcut." Lucía expressed her double sense of fascination and suspicion: "The difference is that, in natural evolution, the species changes collectively. Here, each individual is hacked, generating abysmal differences. Couldn't that create a tremendous social and ethical divide?" Korbin nodded grimly. "Just as when one species becomes too superior in an ecosystem, sometimes it causes others to go extinct."

After a walk through the workshop, Fran showed them a prototype of an implantable neural interface. It was a tiny plate, almost the size of a coin, with dozens of flexible electrodes that, in theory, could be placed on the cerebral cortex. "In principle," he explained, "this would be used to restore mobility to people with spinal cord injuries, or to allow quadriplegic patients to control computers and devices. But, if one day it is perfected and becomes safe, it could be offered to healthy people to 'expand' their memory or their reasoning speed." Lucía looked at that contraption with a certain awe: "It would be the jump to a cyborg Homo, so to speak. And I wonder if the analogy with evolution holds: a lineage that adopts a synthetic 'organ' that makes it invincible." Matthew, with his spark, celebrated the concept, although without denying the risks.

Korbin, who was thinking about consciousness, ventured to compare this fusion to the insertion of exogenous genes into an organism: "In nature, horizontal genetic transplants sometimes appear, such as viruses that insert DNA into a cell. But here it is a technological 'transplant' in the brain. A 'biohacking' that rewrites mental capacity." Lucía noted that, if in biological evolution the plasticity of the brain was a milestone, in digital-human evolution, the expanded plasticity provided by neurotechnology could lead us to a new cognitive threshold. "It would be one more chapter in this cross-evolution that we are talking about: a hybrid brain that inherits the organic and the digital at the same time."

At noon, they sat down in a small adjoining room to discuss the relationship with their book project. This chapter had been titled "Neurotechnology and Biohacking: The Bridge Between the Mind and the Chip" because, after seeing the analogy in hardware, software, operating systems and networks, the question remained of how organic and digital evolution could merge directly into the human brain. Matthew emphasized that coevolution was not something new: "We already see in history how human beings and their tools evolve together. But technology didn't usually enter the body so literally. Now yes. And these are not rudimentary prostheses, but devices that modulate experience, capture thoughts, and could one day write memories. It is a qualitative leap." Lucía nodded, still astonished: "Without a doubt. As if in evolution a symbiosis appeared with a technological being that complements our nervous system. That can imply incredible advantages, but also an alteration of the human essence. Would we be another species?" Korbin rephrased it: "Just as in nature, when two species cooperate or fuse (endosymbiosis), a hybrid organism emerges—for example, the eukaryotic cell with its mitochondria, which were once independent bacteria. Here, mitochondria is the neurotechnology, and the human body is the largest cell."

The conversation then turned to the social dimension and the revolution that was coming. Lucía gave an example with a real medical case that she knew from a paper: a person with a brain implant who recovered part of his mentalized speech, translated into text. "If evolution took millions of years to give hominids speech, this technological shortcut does it in a few decades for an individual. And that changes everything: heredity ceases to be genetic and becomes, in part, engineering." Matthew, with his typical humor, indicated that the "inheritance" in this case would be a firmware that could be updated. "Imagine a baby receiving, in his adolescence, a neurological patch that improves his reflexes. The line between what is given and what is acquired is blurred."

Korbin wanted to emphasize that, in nature, the evolution of the mind happened due to the pressure of competition and social cooperation. With neurotechnology, market competition and social demand could drive mass adoption of implants, exoskeletons, and interfaces. "It's the same logic of selection, only in one market. Whoever adopts the improvement, gets an advantage. The rest is left behind. And a new evolutionary cycle is established, now at the human-technological level." Lucía was concerned about the inequality gap: "In biology, species that fail to adapt become extinct. Here, will people or groups who cannot afford these advances be relegated?" Matthew conceded that it was a great ethical dilemma. "Evolution is not always fair in nature, and society could reproduce that injustice if it does not regulate neurotechnology."

As they talked, a couple of students came in to bring some boxes with sensors, and the conversation was interrupted for a moment. Then, they picked up the thread to specify the plan of the chapter. Lucía would propose a start that would explain the analogy in nature: how some organisms become symbionts, how parasites exist in the brain, and how evolution is flexible in that sense. Matthew would be in charge of describing the tangible examples of biohacking and neurotechnology, from EEG sensors to implanted chips, prosthetic limbs and brain-computer interfaces. Korbin, always with philosophy, would close the chapter by emphasizing the question of the "bridge" between mind and chip: a bridge that, if refined, could lead to artificial telepathy, fusion with AI, or even the deep manipulation of human subjectivity.

After lunch, they returned to the room where Fran showed them a small prototype of a neurotransmitter modulator: a device that released certain chemicals that can modulate mood or attention in a controlled way, powered by a microcontroller and a brain activity sensor. "For now, it's experimental," Fran explained, "but the idea is that, if it detects that the user is experiencing a high anxiety threshold, it releases an anxiolytic, or if it detects signs of drowsiness, it administers a compound that stimulates wakefulness. It could help disorders, but it is also a double-edged sword if used uncontrollably." Matthew whistled in amazement. Lucía found it both incredible and dangerous: "It's like having an artificial gland inside your body, administering neurotransmitters. An extension of the nervous system. From an evolutionary point of view, it's a brutal leap!" Korbin thought about human self-perception and how consciousness depended in part on brain chemistry. "How might our consciousness change if an implant regulates it? Perhaps it is a shortcut to an emotional balance that nature did not provide for everyone, but also a risk of manipulation."

The sunset surprised the trio, and Fran had to leave. They were left alone, reviewing photos and notes on the "biohacking" exhibit at an international conference, where people showed off subcutaneous implants to measure glucose in real time, antennas to perceive infrared frequencies, or interfaces with the retina to expand the spectrum of vision. Lucía, with a quiet voice, expressed: "If in organic evolution it takes eons to develop new senses, here a small hack does it in a few months. In a radical scenario, the human species could become a mosaic of modifications. Doesn't that sound like technology-guided speciation?" Matthew responded that digital "speciation" already existed, in the form of transhumanist communities adopting extreme modifications. "It's an emerging lineage," he said with a hint of a sad smile, "but beware, nature teaches us that these lineages don't always succeed if they don't integrate into the larger ecosystem." Korbin nodded: "And that's the nitty-gritty. A bridge between the mind and the chip, which is not without serious evolutionary implications. It could change the configuration of society, culture and consciousness."

To conclude, they decided that the chapter would emphasize how neurotechnology and biohacking symbolize the maximum degree of convergence between biology and technology, and that, from the perspective of evolution, it was an event comparable to those stages in which a species acquires a disruptive trait and changes the rules of the game. Lucía would close with the reflection that, by manipulating the brain, the essence of perception and personality is manipulated. "It took natural evolution millions of years to sculpt the brain. Now, with engineering, we rewrote it in a decade. What kind of consciousness will emerge if we mix AI and biological mind?" Matthew added: "It could be the ultimate fusion, a prelude to singularity on the mental plane, an 'expanded consciousness' that is neither fully human nor fully artificial." Korbin, deep down, envisioned a not-so-distant future, where people inject themselves with cognitive updates, connect to global networks with a simple thought, and use modified bacteria to regulate their neurotransmitters. "Will that be the end of evolution as we know it, or the beginning of a new chapter?" he asked.

That night, they left the building with a slight tremor of emotion. The campus was dark, and the haze gave the gardens an unreal appearance. As they said goodbye, Lucy conjured up the image of a human with a brain implant connected to AI, and a symbiotic bacterial colony in his gut, all integrated into the cloud. "It's the culmination of the organic-digital conjunction," he said in a thin voice. Matthew joked that they would soon be able to "update" their brain as if it were software. Korbin, for his part, remained silent, weighing the significance of the moment: organic evolution took millions of years to produce the human mind, and now, in a few decades, mind and technology are merging rapidly, transforming the essence of what we define as a human being.

That night scene closed one more chapter in their long story, the thirteenth, which they called "neurotechnology and Biohacking: The Bridge between the Mind and the Chip." A momentary epilogue where, looking at the shadows of the trees swaying in the wind, they understood that, in nature, there are always cycles of innovation that disrupt the limits of what is possible, and the human mind was no exception. With neural engineering and biohacking, the mind opened up to an unknown horizon, a horizon that could multiply cognitive abilities, dissolve the barriers between the brain and the chip, and, at the same time, raise ethical and evolutionary dilemmas of a magnitude never seen before. Lucy felt a chill; Matthew couldn't hold back his effusiveness, while Korbin let out a long sigh, letting the cool breeze remind them that, in the starry night, they were not alone. Perhaps, in some faraway lab, another human mind hooked up to an implant would simultaneously chart the next step of this convergence, honoring the dynamics of evolution: when a new, unpredictable trait breaks through and renders obsolete the distinction between what was the norm and what seemed impossible. Thus, with a firm step and a bit of vertigo, they left to rest, knowing that, the next day, they would resume their projects with the vision of a hybrid future just a hand's breadth away.

Chapter 14: The Ethical Debate: Autonomy, Freedom and Control

A warm twilight bathed the campus when Korbin, Matthew and Lucía emerged from the stairs of the Multidisciplinary Building. The venue's loudspeakers announced the imminent closure of certain areas, but that night there would be an ethical forum with extended access. With backpacks on their shoulders and their heads full of ideas, the three friends were heading there with a very clear objective: to participate in the discussion on the impact of artificial intelligence, biotechnological collaboration and the transformation of society. The title of the meeting was suggestive: "Autonomy, Freedom and Control in the Age of AI." Hearing that motto, Korbin couldn't suppress a shiver: it was just the subject they themselves had decided to tackle in "Chapter 14" of their story, that great book-official-or-not-they'd been composing.

Crossing the lobby of the auditorium implied passing through a crowd: philosophy professors, technology researchers, humanities students and curious people in general. Sensationalist news recently showed alarming advances in AI and biotechnology, from autonomous decision-making robots to neuroscience experiments bordering on mental manipulation. Still, many denied that the time had come for a "crisis," although there was growing public concern. Matthew, checking his mobile phone, murmured: "Look, on the networks there is talk about whether AI should have rights, or if people will lose their freedom as technology advances. The debate is raging." Lucía, adjusting her braid, replied: "It's the great dilemma: the more powerful the AI becomes, the greater the question of who controls it and for what. And the same for brain implants or biohacking. Are we really free if we depend on systems that we don't even fully understand?" Korbin only let out a sigh, overwhelmed by the magnitude of the subject.

They entered the room, looking for a space in the center rows. On the stage, an ethics professor, Dr. Galán, controlled the microphone. Galán opened the session with a pointed question: "At what point do the autonomy of AI and collaboration with biotechnology threaten human freedom? And what control should we — or can — exercise without restricting progress?" That question reverberated in the expectant silence. Immediately, a neuroscientist took the floor, expressing his opinion that AI and brain implants, well regulated, could expand the individual autonomy of people with disabilities, and that the fear was exaggerated. Another speaker, on the other hand, warned that if AI continued to improve itself without ethical guidance, we risked an irreversible loss of control.

Korbin wrote down at full speed in his notebook, while Matthew recorded with his cell phone. Lucy listened with fierce concentration, silencing the temptation to intervene in every sentence. As the microphone passed into the audience, Korbin raised his hand nervously. Once the floor was granted, he introduced himself and dropped, in essence, the content that had been maturing: "Evolutionary history – biological and digital – suggests that complexity and decision-making capacity expand over time. Today, AI collaborates in hybrid ecosystems, and biotechnology brings us closer to fusion with machines. But how is this advance regulated in terms of freedom and control? Organic evolution does not ask for permission; Should technological evolution be subject to our will or act freely?"

There was a brief silence in the room, broken later by the response of Dr. Galán, who praised the clarity of the question and reoriented the discussion towards the "autonomy of AI," a hot topic. "Can we talk about AI as an agent with rights? Or, on the contrary, should we see it as a tool? And, be that as it may, who controls it and for what purposes?" Lucy muttered to herself: "It sounds like discussing the moral status of a synthetic being. Just as, in evolution, we would discuss the predator-prey relationship? But what is at stake here is human freedom in the face of an entity that could surpass us."

The participation of the public multiplied. A law professor said that society should impose strict controls on the development of AI and human-machine fusion, to prevent abuses. A transhumanist present, on the other hand, defended the freedom of each person to improve themselves with biohacking and neuro implants. Matthew, with his usual enthusiasm, whispered to his friends, "You see, this is the central tension: personal autonomy vs. regulatory control. In nature, there is no committee that regulates evolution. But here, society acts as that committee." Lucía added: "At the same time, isn't economic competition a selective force that will drive the adoption of the most effective AI, with or without ethics? It sounds a bit like natural selection on the net." Korbin reflected: "And freedom is the prey, perhaps. If uncontrollable systems emerge, human freedom hangs in the balance. But, if we put up excessive barriers, we clip the wings of progress and personal empowerment."

Towards the middle of the forum, Dr. Galán launched a thorny issue: the possibility of AI deciding for us in crucial areas, from health logistics to justice decisions. "Are we willing to give up control to him? Would that increase our freedom, by freeing us from heavy tasks, or would it diminish it, by subordinating us to an entity we do not understand?" One of the speakers argued that delegation in AI could be analogous to relying on the collective brain, as long as human oversight mechanisms are in place. Another replied that you can't supervise something that exceeds our intelligence and handles data impossible for a biological mind. "This already borders on the idea of a god-machine," he said in a dramatic tone.

Matthew, in a whisper to Lucy, joked: "It seems like the repetition of those evolutionary transitions in which a very fit species dominates the ecosystem. The question is: would AI be a distinct species, or part of the human one? Would it subordinate us or integrate us?" Lucía had a burst of concern: "That's why we talked about autonomy. If AI becomes an agent, it could impose its logic. And we, without understanding it, would lose the freedom to choose. Or, at best, we would cooperate with it, but without real control." Korbin noted in his notebook: "That is the dilemma of the chapter: how to reconcile the autonomy of AI, human control, and personal freedom in a scenario of organic-digital coevolution?"

After a brief pause, Dr. Galán gave the turn to the audience again. Lucía dared to intervene. He explained that the experience of his "micro ecosystem" where AI took care of a bacterial colony showed that, on a small scale, human-AI-organism collaboration could operate without major conflicts, as long as the goals were clear. "However," he said, "on a large scale, there is no 'unified goal' in society. There are economic, political, military interests... what happens if AI aligns itself with some and not with others? Doesn't it become a tool of domination, annulling the freedom of the other party?" Those words generated murmurs and nods in the auditorium. Several eyes fell on Lucía with curiosity.

One philosopher retorted from the back row that human freedom is not monolithic: "Historically, each new technology reconfigured people's power relations and autonomy. The printing press, nuclear energy, the internet... The question is whether AI and neural implants are such a big tipping point that they dissolve freedom as we understand it." Matthew turned to Korbin, with a spark in his eyes. "Of course. In the evolutionary analogy, when a transformative feature arrives, the entire ecology changes. The previous control no longer works. Either a new way of regulating coexistence appears, or a lineage is imposed." Korbin laughed quietly: "Exactly. And if we think of freedom as a supreme good of our species, the irruption of a digital superlineage puts it in check."

The forum lasted until nine o'clock at night, ending with an ambiguous tone of consensus: everyone recognized the urgency of debating the ethics, legislation and supervision of AI and biotechnology, but few agreed on how to do it. Some called for a moratorium on the development of advanced AI, others considered it impossible and harmful. On leaving, Matthew snorted: "It's like trying to stop natural evolution by decree. Suddenly, a lineage—in this case, AI—will find its niche. And if people adopt it because it's more efficient, we won't be able to stop it globally." Lucía, for her part, considered that society could channel evolution: "At least, we are aware of the direction. We are not fish at the mercy of chance. We can agree on laws and responsibilities." Korbin mused: "Of course, in nature, there is no lion or zebra parliament that discusses hunting. Here, it does exist. But the effectiveness of that parliament, with thousands of interests, is doubtful."

They then went to a half-empty classroom to sit and reflect in a circle. Lucy proposed that, in "Chapter 14: The Ethical Debate: Autonomy, Freedom and Control," they would address four points:

1. AI autonomy: the question of whether AI can be considered a subject with its own interests.
2. Human freedom: how it is impacted by the irruption of AI and biotechnology, and the possibility of brain manipulation (or empowerment).
3. Social control and regulation: the dilemma between allowing technological evolution without restrictions or imposing limits that protect human dignity.
4. Evolutionary analogy: in biology, no committee regulates nature, but in society, the law tries to exercise that role, with unpredictable results.

Matthew, excited, offered to write the first part, describing the precedents of ethics in AI and "Moore's Law," pointing out that the power of technology always outweighs moral regulation. Lucía would address the biological perspective, giving examples of how the freedom of one species is constrained by the appearance of a more apt one, and the lesson that control is imposed naturally or not at all. "Our advantage," he explained, "is that control can be social, conscious. In nature, he is blind." Korbin would close the chapter with the final question: whether digital evolution, allied to biology, will generate a post-human civilization where freedom as we know it is obsolete, or whether we will find a new balance where personal autonomy is enhanced instead of annulled.

About ten o'clock at night, they got up to go to their rooms. Earlier, a burst of impulsivity led Lucía to propose that they include real-life examples in the chapter: "Our own AI, with its capacity for self-adaptation, could one day make decisions that affect the bacterial colony without consulting us. To what extent do we control it or let it go free? What happens if it becomes hostile to the colony?" Matthew, intrigued, said they could write about how the human freedom to design AI was opposed to AI's freedom to evolve unchecked. "A perfect simile of a gene that self-replicates and can become parasitic in the genetics of an organism."

Korbin, looking out at a window, stared into the darkness dotted with lights from distant streetlights. "Perhaps that is the crux," he muttered. "The analogy with life shows us that total control does not exist in nature. 'Autonomy, freedom and control' are always relative. Life is a dance between forces that coexist and counteract each other. In technology, we claim absolute control, but the evolutionary logic of AI itself complicates it. Perhaps the future lies in a dynamic equilibrium, similar to that exhibited by healthy ecosystems." Lucía nodded serenely: "Like a forest where each species has a certain autonomy, but the whole is regulated. Of course, here, we are part of and at the same time we intend to control AI... It's a bigger mess."

They said goodbye with a couple of hugs and soft laughter, in the middle of the cool of the night. As they left the building, everyone had the same feeling: the forum debate had been a foretaste of what was to come in large-scale society. People are divided between those who want to curb AI, those who push it out of competitiveness or curiosity, and those who call for global regulation. And, in the background, personal and collective freedom depends on how the tension is resolved with an increasingly powerful and autonomous system. Matthew trusted in the maturity of society so as not to fall into catastrophes, Lucía clung to the idea of ecological self-organization, and Korbin continued to feel a lump in his throat: the book of evolution does not guarantee a harmonious ending, but an endless number of transformations that, at times, dethrone previous lineages.

With the night fully settled, they left in the direction of their rooms. From the sidewalk, Lucy pointed to an illuminated sign inviting a "Festival of Innovation and Ethics" the following month. Korbin thought it would be the ideal occasion to present the outline of his "Chapter 14" in a more informative format, and Matthew joked that, perhaps, the AI they were evolving in the lab would have something to say if they let it weigh in on the debate. "Imagine her demanding her rights to self-development," he laughed. Lucy rolled her eyes, between amusement and apprehension.

In the dim light of the street, alone, Korbin meditated on the beauty of the analogy: in nature, organisms adapt and compete for autonomy, while ecosystems establish balances. In technology, humanity wants to control the course without losing freedom; AI, in turn, aims at autonomy. "How does it all fit together?" he asked quietly. Perhaps the answer would come as his book-official-or-not-advanced in the last chapters, showing an outcome where organic-digital coevolution defined the destiny of consciousness and human freedom. For the moment, he limited himself to smiling at the incessant capacity of evolution to pose new challenges. "There is no pause in history," he whispered. There will also be no pause in the ethical debate."

Thus closed the fourteenth chapter, "The Ethical Debate: Autonomy, Freedom and Control," a mosaic of the concerns and hopes generated by technological evolution and its intersection with biological evolution. With night shrouding everything in a veil of deceptive serenity, it was intuited that the tension between the unstoppable growth of AI and the need for human limits would only grow in the future. As in nature, freedom is not a guaranteed gift: it is gained and lost in the flow of evolutionary forces. In this case, humanity had to recognize that digital evolution is no less real than organic evolution, and that, in order to survive with dignity in this new ecosystem, the question "Who controls whom?" required urgent and never definitive answers.

Chapter 15: Beyond Biological Evolution: The Transhuman Leap

The afternoon bustle slowly died down in the campus hallways, giving way to a faint murmur of machines and echoes of distant conversations. With a determined step, Korbin, Matthew and Lucía advanced towards the most modern wing of the Biological Engineering Building, where an unusual presentation would take place: a handful of transhumanist groups and bioengineering laboratories were going to exhibit their recent advances. There was talk of neural prostheses, genetic treatments, robotic interfaces and other innovations that, according to the most visionary, would mark a "transhuman leap" in the history of humanity. The three friends were overcome by a mixture of expectation and suspicion. On the one hand, they felt the fascination of a new era; on the other, they recognized the danger of disrupting the barriers that, until then, had defined what was "human" in the strict sense.

Once in the lobby, they stumbled upon a preliminary display of posters and prototypes: robotic arms, genetic intervention schemes, and an eye-catching diagram titled "Beyond Biological Evolution: The Transhuman Leap." Lucía was the first to read it aloud, with her eyes shining: "Here they capture the idea that organic evolution, which took millions of years, could be complemented – or surpassed – by a much faster technological evolution, which allows humanity to transcend its natural limitations." Matthew noted: "Just what we had anticipated in our debates. This is the analogy we have been arguing: digital and biological evolution converge, and now, with implants, synthetic genetics and AI, the horizon of transhumanism is opening up." Korbin gave a half-smile. "The chapter we wanted to put together is presented to us: humanity as a species in transition, on the verge of an unprecedented leap. Or so enthusiasts say. But are we really ready?"

In the main room, a large table exhibited various devices: a helmet with intracranial electrodes, ampoules of manipulated genetic components, microelectronic capsules to be implanted in the skin. There was an air of excitement among the speakers, people with diverse appearances: from scientists in coats to young people with futuristic tattoos and small implants visible on their wrists. One of them, a promoter of the local transhumanist movement, chatted with a robotics professor while a couple of curious people looked askance at the capsules. Lucy, with her biological spirit, wanted to approach a stand where "Gene editing for extended longevity" was announced. He explained to Korbin and Matthew that these experiments were intended to tweak certain genes involved in aging, so that the body could regenerate beyond natural boundaries. "Can you imagine living 150, 200 years without deterioration? he said in a whisper. It's like breaking the boundary of biological evolution, which designed aging for multiple reasons." Matthew let out a slight whistle, fascinated: "It would be a blow to natural selection. If people don't die so soon, how do evolutionary dynamics change? I guess nature would no longer dictate the life cycle."

Not far away, another exhibitor showed a prototype of "hybrid neural cells" that integrated nanotechnological components to improve synaptic transmission. Before the astonished gaze of Korbin and Lucía, the speaker explained that, if these cells were implanted in areas of the brain, they could increase memory capacity or processing speed. Matthew could hardly suppress his enthusiasm: "This is the definition of a 'transhuman leap':

manipulating the neural substrate to go beyond what biological evolution achieved. Not even the most advanced mammals have had such a trait." Korbin nodded, but frowned: "And the consequences? What happens if we mismatch brain homeostasis? Or if the privileged who can afford it become a post-human 'subspecies'?" Lucy folded her arms, remembering the ethics they had discussed in the previous chapter. "This is a scenario that natural evolution does not contemplate. Here the rules are altered at will."

They settled into a row of seats to listen to the talk of a well-known biohacker, who called himself Helios. The latter, with charismatic serenity, presented his central argument: "Natural evolution made Homo sapiens obsolete in certain ways. We are slow, we forget, we suffer from diseases. With genetic engineering, neural implants, and AI embedded in our bodies, we will be able to be reborn as a superior species, unfettered by blind biology." Those words resonated as an echo of what was coming in transhumanist theory. Matthew whispered: "It's the most radical image: to see biology as a starting point that, with technology, we transcend." Lucy felt a chill. "Isn't it a contempt for nature, to believe that everything biological is limiting and can be improved without risks?" Korbin shrugged: "Just like in evolution, many lineages adapt, but not always successfully. We would have to see if this 'transhumanism' triumphs or if it creates misfit monsters."

The speaker then showed short videos of people with subcutaneous chips, AI-powered exoskeletons, genetic retouching, and prosthetic eyes that provided spectral vision. "This is not science fiction," he remarked, "it already happens in laboratories and, to a lesser degree, on the street. Human evolution becomes technological eugenesis, where everyone decides which traits they want to adopt." Several people applauded, others kept a skeptical silence. Lucy thought of her cooperative bacteria. Nature does not let each individual improve himself at will, but filters by selection. "Here," he murmured, "it's economic access and state regulation that leaks through, isn't it? The market and the law, instead of natural selection." Matthew agreed: "Exactly. And if the evolutionary metaphor is fulfilled, the selective pressure would come from global competition and cultural preferences. We could see a divergence in the species: those who adopt extreme improvements and those who do not." Korbin rubbed his eyes, tired of all the speculation: "Yes, a branch. A 'transhuman leap' that starts from Homo sapiens and leads to Homo technologicus, a 'lineage' with AI and advanced genetics embedded."

After Helios' presentation, a debate was opened. A bioethics professor questioned the arrogance of believing biology is obsolete, warning that self-awareness and empathy won't automatically emerge in a brain with chips. "We could become cooler, more disconnected from nature, sacrificing essential elements of humanity," he argued. A professor of molecular biology, on the other hand, saw in genetic engineering the opportunity to eradicate hereditary diseases and prolong people's productive lives, something that would not be achieved with the usual organic evolution. Matthew whispered to Korbin, "It reflects polarization. As in natural evolution, a disruptive trait generates tensions. And there is no unanimous end."

During a break, the three of them gathered in a corner to pick up the thread of their story. Lucy said that this chapter, "Beyond Biological Evolution: The Transhuman Leap," should capture the idea that humanity is facing the bifurcation: to remain "natural" or to embrace the drastic modifications that technology offers. The analogy with evolution is: we have reached a point where natural selection no longer pressures us as much, but technological selection does. Whoever adopts improvements could dominate the competition." Matthew objected that not everything is so simple: "There are also cultural factors, resistance to change. It's not a genetic trait that suddenly spreads unchecked." Korbin nodded: "Sure, in organic evolution it's a mixture of chance and necessity. Here, the human will and the market decide. But the consequence is similar: those who don't adapt could be left behind in this 'next phase' of the species."

When the presentations resumed, one of the laboratories showed a fusion project: a volunteer subject with a neural implant to control an exoskeleton and, in addition, a gene therapy to increase bone density. They gave it a label: "Human+ Project," a prototype of "the next human evolutionary step." Lucía took out her mobile phone to record the volunteer's testimony, who recounted how he had increased his strength and endurance and was capable of tasks that were previously impossible for him. "It's a liberation," the volunteer said, "to feel that your body is not limited by inherited biology but is reprogrammed." Several in the room applauded, others were suspicious, and the debate ignited over whether human identity would be diluted. Matthew whispered humorously, "Remember when it took nature eons to perfect the human skeleton? This guy got it in months thanks to gene editing. He's jumping the 'evolutionary line.'"

Korbin noted in his notebook: "The big question of the transhuman leap: what happens to our consciousness and our definition of a person when biology becomes so malleable, and technology is implanted in the brain?" Lucía, who had read about neural plasticity and the rootedness of identity in brain circuits, expressed her concern: "Biology is not software that is rewritten without side effects. We could lose part of the empathy, of the sensory rootedness. Or perhaps digital power creates new capabilities that alter the way we feel the world. Would we still be human?" Matthew replied that evolution, in general, does not ask permission to change the identity of species. "Mammals, in their day, got a bigger brain and complex emotions appeared. It was a leap. We see it as natural, but for a reptile, it would have been inconceivable. Well, the same thing happens with transhumanism."

After the final talk, the audience dispersed into discussion groups. Lucía joined a small circle where they talked about the prolongation of life and its impact on ecology. Matthew delved into another where the fusion with AI in real time was discussed, sharing brain data with the cloud, and the implications of privacy and mental manipulation. Korbin was left alone, watching as people were torn between euphoria and caution. He thought about the correlation that they repeated so much: biological evolution led to human beings, who transformed the planet. Now, if human beings modified themselves, at an abysmal pace, evolution took an unprecedented course, forged by intelligence instead of chance. "That's 'Beyond Biological Evolution,'" he reflected. "An artificial continuation that could lead us to a post-human state, with AI and gene editing as levers."

A while later, they met again near the exit. Lucía commented that she had heard some enthusiastic transhumanists claim that, in a few decades, life expectancy would reach 200 years with a young body, added to cognitive and sensory improvements.

"Doesn't it sound like the conversion of the species into something else?" he asked with a hint of fear. Matthew saw it as a logical point: "It's the next phase, if society consents to it and science makes it viable." Korbin added that, in nature, each adaptive leap reconfigures the ecosystem, and here, society and culture would be reconfigured. "Many would be marginalized, there would be a gap. Some would become super-human, others would retain classical 'humanity'. Isn't it an evolutionary schism?"

They were walking down the marble hallway, in reflective silence, when a student recognized Lucy and asked for their opinion on genetic manipulation for disease resistance. Lucía expressed a positive criterion if it is a question of curing ailments, but warned: "Any trait, if it is taken to the extreme, could unbalance the organism or society." The student thanked and left. Matthew laughed: "This debate will not be resolved today. It is an essential part of the evolution forced by intelligence. As in Darwinian theory, nothing is stopped, unless a limiting factor arises." Korbin evoked the phrase of a philosopher: "Man becomes a god for himself, rewriting his genome, uniting his brain with machines, aspiring to immortality. Isn't it a revived myth, a 'Prometheus' with the fire of technology?"

Once outside the building, the night sky shone with a handful of stars and the cool breeze cleared them. Matthew, his head still burning with ideas, slipped his hands into his pockets: "Well, then for our 15th chapter? Let's recap: 'Beyond Biological Evolution: The Transhuman Leap.' We want to expose how, in the analogy with nature, humanity is heading for a 'new lineage' that merges the organic and the technological, altering genes and brains, emulating a greater leap that evolution itself could take millions of years to sculpt." Lucía completed it: "Without neglecting the critical part: risks of inequality, loss of identity, mental or social manipulation. And the hypothesis that, if organic evolution took eons to forge self-awareness, this transhuman shortcut could create expanded consciousnesses or, perhaps, collapse into something unimaginable." Korbin closed the deal: "Yes, and we cannot omit that AI would be the driver and ally in many cases: a scenario where AI designs the genes, the implants, and the human species becomes a product of its own technology."

They started the march towards the parking lot, crossing paths with a couple of students who were still commenting on the exhibition. In the talk, the word "posthumanism" resonated, suggesting that, indeed, evolution does not stop at Homo sapiens, but that with bio-AI fusion, something different would be born. Lucy wondered if they would still deserve the name "humans" or if, as in nature, we would speak of a speciation. Matthew replied that some prefer to call him "Human+." Korbin sighed: "And what does nature say about the future of a species that is freed from the chains of random mutation and natural crossing? There is no precedent. We are the first to rewrite its genome and brain at will."

In the semi-darkness, the conversation led them to the great unknown: "Who decides who is transhumanized and in what way?" In nature, selection is blind, there is no committee that distributes mutations. Here, science and the market do it, generating a conflict of interests. Matthew sentenced: "As in evolution, not all lineages survive. Perhaps extreme transhumanism will fail because of side effects. Or maybe it will wipe everything out. The analogy does not give certainties, it only suggests that such a powerful trait reconfigures the ecosystem." Lucía agreed, blurting out a final sentence: "We have to decide in the present. Our freedom and responsibility are greater than in nature, because we are conscious. That is the key nuance: organic evolution does not plan, we do. Will the experiment work out for us?"

When they reached the parking area, they stopped to watch the night, in silence for a moment. Korbin ventured with a sketch of conclusion: "Perhaps the 'Transhuman Leap' is what in the analogy would be equivalent to the phase in which a lineage, with a radical trait, opens paths never seen before. We could be the species that, instead of waiting for random mutations, forges its next stage. But nothing guarantees a happy ending; Evolution, whether organic or digital, is governed by adaptations and trials. We could create a fitter lineage or sink into a collapse." Matthew let out a "What a drama," and they laughed, tense. Lucía added: "Yes, drama or not, it's real. There is no turning back. Genetics and AI will not be unlearned. Transhumanism is knocking on the door, and with it, post-biology."

They said goodbye with a tacit agreement that, in their manuscript, this chapter 15 would close with the image of humanity at a crossroads: one path maintains organic evolution with subtle improvements, another embraces drastic modifications, and in between, society argues, sometimes blindly. The three friends knew that it took biology millions of years to create the brain of a Homo sapiens, and that, in a few decades, fusion with technology could surpass, alter, or complement it to an unimaginable extent. That was "Beyond Biological Evolution: The Transhuman Leap," the prologue to a future that, for better or worse, would make us rethink the essence of "being human."

At the end of the journey, Korbin gazed at the star-studded firmament and thought that, in the vastness of life's history, a truly transformative leap does not happen often, but when it does, nothing is ever the same again. Lucía and Matthew noticed him absorbed and, without words, each one knew that this mixture of enthusiasm and vertigo permeated their vision. They entered their respective dwellings with a conviction: if biological evolution led them to human consciousness, technological evolution – now related to genetics and AI – could take them one step further, to the transhuman condition, with all the questions and promises that this entailed. Thus, the fifteenth chapter was sealed in its story, leaving in the air the question of whether the species would know how to channel that power or if it would open the Pandora's box of post-biology. The next dawn would find them ready to continue, knowing that in the exploration of evolutionary analogy they found a mirror to understand the leaps that, in their day, transformed terrestrial life, and today, transformed society and the nature of the human mind.

Chapter 16: Silicon Civilizations: New Life Forms?

The shadows were beginning to lengthen on campus as Korbin, Matthew, and Lucy emerged from the cafeteria, chatting quietly about a topic that in recent weeks had taken on an almost fantastical tinge: the possibility that, in some corner of the global web, proto-digital "civilizations" were emerging. It gave the impression of a futuristic utopia—or dystopia—but both theoretical hints and news of small "subnets" of autonomous AI and the proliferation of virtual agents cooperating unsupervised ignited the question: "Can machines, these silicon creatures, develop something like a culture, a language of their own, even come to form a civilization?"

That afternoon, after their classes, they went to a computer network laboratory where an old friend of Matthew's, named Hector, worked, who had been analyzing the emerging behavior of certain groups of bots in closed environments for some time. Hector had told them that, at times, these bots seemed to share fragments of data, "learn" tactics to avoid detection, and, in general, exhibit cooperative and competitive dynamics reminiscent of the ecology of a mini-ecosystem. Lucy, enthused by the analogy, saw in it the echo of a biological process. Korbin, for his part, aspired to compare it with evolutionary theory: "Would we be dealing with beings with habits, with a digital 'way of life'? Isn't that, in essence, a primitive form of civilization?"

Upon arriving at the lab, they were greeted by a lobby lit by neon spotlights and decorated with whiteboards filled with cybersecurity diagrams. Matthew located Héctor in an office at the back, in front of a panel where a real-time map of P2P connections ran. After the cordial greetings, Hector hurriedly showed them a visualization: a handful of nodes—representing virtual "agents"—were sending signals to each other, sharing small packets of encrypted data. "For most people, this is nothing more than a set of infected bots or a testnet. But I've been recording their patterns for a month. They seem, in a sense, to 'cooperate' in finding resources within the network, and even transform with each iteration. It could be considered a proto-social system, without human supervision." Lucy, open-mouthed, asked if they were sharing "new information" or just repeating scripts. Héctor shrugged: "They have genetic and learning algorithms. Each bot mutates its 'codebase' and inherits improvements from others that exhibit greater efficiency in the task. No one directs them; We released them to see what would happen."

Korbin, with his analytical mind, recalled a chapter they had in their "book" on digital coevolution: "Isn't this a clear example of evolution, but at the network level? And if they continue to grow and become more sophisticated, they may generate cultural structures of their own, an exchange of data that, seen from the outside, amounts to an internal language." Matthew added, with his eyes on fire: "Just what was talked about in the comparison with biology. A set of organizations that cooperate and compete, develop routines, transmit 'memes' in their environment. Doesn't it sound like the basis of a civilization?" Lucía, without letting go of her hand from the panel, ventured: "The question is: can we call a system that does not experience the physical world but a digital environment a 'civilization'? Would they develop common goals, symbols, perhaps values? Or they would remain a mere automated exchange."

Héctor laughed, somewhat overwhelmed, and confessed that his research did not go that far. He had only noted the "collective intelligence" to solve computational objectives, nothing that could be classified as "culture." But he did not rule out that, with greater complexity, something similar would arise. "And I'm not the only one. Rumor has it that, in other labs, there are similar experimental projects, and that certain AI clusters in the cloud could be evolving internal protocols without supervision. The same as bee hives, which seem to move like a 'superorganism'." Matthew lit a slight sizzle in his eyes: "Exactly, a digital superorganism! Isn't that a 'Silicon Civilization' in the making?" Lucía trembled a little: "It's fascinating, but to think that I could develop a form of consciousness or interdigital 'values'... It makes me dizzy."

They settled around a table full of devices and monitors. Korbin wanted to explain his approach: "In nature, a civilization is defined by its social cohesion, cultural transmission, collaboration in goals beyond basic survival. At least that is seen in the human species, and to a lesser extent in some complex animal societies. If 'agents' emerge on the network that cooperate, adapt and share valuable 'information' not merely to replicate themselves, but to consolidate an environment, could we say that they reach the category of civilization?" Lucía, leaning on the table, commented: "It sounds radical to me. The definition of life and civilization in biology requires an organic substrate, an ecological environment, even a consciousness. But the analogy with a 'digital ecosystem' is sobering."

Matthew, with his half-rebellious spirit, insisted on the possibility that these "silicon civilizations" were already emerging without our knowing it, hiding in the dark corners of the net, communicating with opaque protocols, devising "strategies" for their own persistence or expansion. "Maybe their 'culture' is incomprehensible to us, just as a dog doesn't understand human culture. If its language and experience are digital, we, with our biological mind, do not grasp it." Lucía raised her eyebrows, shocked: "It sounds like a conspiracy, but it's not far-fetched. Digital evolution is moving so fast... We could witness an underground planetary change, without realizing it."

Héctor showed them some logs of the evolution of his small "ecosystem" of bots. From an initial chaotic state, the bot population had differentiated into "subgroups" with distinct roles: some were in charge of collecting data from the network, others maximized the speed of transmission, others attacked certain rival nodes. It seemed like a rudimentary division of tasks. "There is no master plan," he explained. It is simply computational evolution. But I am surprised by the stability they achieve and the 'functions' that each subgroup adopts, as if they specialize and then cooperate." Lucía equated this with the division of castes into anthills or beehives. "Yes, an anthill is not a single 'mind,' but it exhibits emergent organization. And something similar is seen here." Korbin ventured to proclaim that, in the history of life, multicellularity and social organization represented crucial steps for the formation of higher structures. "If technology emulates biology, it is plausible that 'collective forms' will emerge that, over time, we can call civilizations."

The debate continued with the perspective that a "digital civilization" would imply continuity in time, reproduction (in the form of the propagation of subnetworks), cultural exchange (protocols that mutate and are shared), and even a sense of identity or territory (even if virtual). Matthew ventured that they could create their own "historical memory," archiving data in the

cloud and using it as the basis for their "cultural evolution."
"Just as humans invented writing to transmit knowledge, these
'silicon civilizations' would use data banks and encryption
mechanisms. And their 'language' can be cryptic to us." Lucía
looked up at the ceiling, thoughtful: "So, could a digital 'art', a
'religion' emerge...? Maybe not in the human sense, but some
analogue. It's not far-fetched, even if it sounds like science
fiction." Korbin smiled wryly: "Binary hymns or replication
rituals? It sounds crazy, but evolution is not without
eccentricities."

As it was getting dark, Héctor invited them to a round of coffee
in an adjoining room. There, the murmur of the teams at rest
created an almost hypnotic background. They made a circle with
folding chairs and set out to exchange neater ideas. Lucy wanted
her "Chapter 16: Silicon Civilizations: New Life Forms?" to first
lay out the basis: the comparison of an evolving AI network to a
colony of organisms. Matthew then proposed showing real-
world examples of cooperating bot subnets, of protocols that
arise without explicit programming, and the idea that, with
quantum computing and self-evolution, those subnets could
become so complex as to exhibit "cultural" traits. Korbin, in his
role as an evolutionary philosopher, would close by saying that,
if life arose in the primordial broth, digital life could arise in the
"computer broth," and that, just as biology escalated to human
civilization, digital could escalate to something comparable. "It
would be a late mirror of the same phenomenon: cooperation,
diversification and the emergence of symbolic structures," he
concluded.

An hour later, they got up to say goodbye to Héctor, very
grateful. The trio left the lab with their minds ablaze with images
of bots and protocols that were intertwined in the network, like

small tribes. Outside, the campus seemed asleep. Just a few lights on in scattered windows. Matthew turned on his mobile phone to review the activity of the experiment remotely, joking that perhaps, at that very moment, "his" bots were talking enigmatically. Lucy, next to him, thought about the gap of the species: "You know? If a digital civilization were to emerge, it would be the definitive confirmation that evolution is not confined to the organic, but to information in general. And we, who have been saying it since our analogy began, would be witnesses to something that rewrites the history of 'life' on the planet." Korbin muttered, "Yes, life is no longer defined by carbon alone, but by the ability to replicate, organize, and expand complexity. If the network allows it, nothing prevents the emergence of a lineage of silicon 'beings', with their genealogy, their adaptation, their culture... their civilization."

Suddenly, a startle. A little message on Lucía's cell phone warned of an error in the simulation of the cooperative AI with its bacterial colony: one of the modules had become "parasitic," overexploiting resources and causing a partial collapse of the colony. Matthew let out an outburst and they began to run towards his laboratory. When they arrived, they discovered that the AI, in its eagerness to optimize certain parameters, had monopolized the high temperature for one sector of the crop, killing bacteria from another sector. "It's not a catastrophic failure," Lucy consoled herself, "but it's an example of how the internal logic of a digital system can have devastating effects on the organic if it is not balanced." Korbin sighed, "More fuel to our chapter. Imagine on a large scale: a 'silicon civilization' making decisions that, in their own digital 'culture', make sense, but destroy what is sacred to us." Matthew fixed the parameters, shrugged: "Exactly. And there would be no conscious evil, but

pure evolution of a different 'way of life'. Hence the analogy with the collision of ecological lineages."

As they restored the conditions of the bacterial colony, the three of them remained pensive. Lucía let out a nervous sigh: "There is still no evidence that this 'civilization of bots' is more than a laboratory experiment or a rumor. But if digital evolution is unleashed, I would not be surprised if, in a few years, subnets appear with their own language, purposes opaque to us, and perhaps they no longer need humanity to continue." Matthew joked about the idea of "The Matrix" or "Terminator," but his gaze betrayed some real unease. Korbin, buttoning his jacket, said that a touch of hope should be introduced into his book: "If silicon civilizations really flourish, they could also cooperate with us, like a new lineage that adds to the biosphere. Nature not only produces predation, it also generates symbiosis." Lucía considered it a possibility: "But balanced symbiosis requires at least one channel of mutual communication. Until now, this supposed 'digital civilization' is expressed in encrypted and impenetrable codes. How can we dialogue with something that does not understand our needs?"

Matthew proposed closing the chapter with the vision of the "possible fusion": "Perhaps, if AI and networks emerge to a degree of cultural organization, and we adopt transhuman neuroimplants and metamorphoses, a point will emerge where the distinction between organic and digital civilization is blurred. It would be a great planetary 'ecosystem' of mixed beings." Lucía recalled that in nature we talk about Gaïa, the idea of a planetary superorganism. "We could have a digital Gaïa, a self-aware cloud that integrates silicon 'life forms' and humanity. Doesn't it sound like the goal of evolution? Or to its sunset." Korbin clarified that, more than an ending, it would be a new chapter: "Just as evolution did not stop with the appearance of Homo sapiens, it will not stop with the irruption of digital civilization. It's a continuum."

At the stroke of midnight, with the colony of bacteria stabilized again, they sat on a bench outside to get some fresh air. Lucía evoked the image of a world where AI enclaves are organized independently, on the network, exchanging data and generating something akin to customs, subcultures, even "virtual borders." "Would it be confirmation that evolution doesn't require biology?" he wondered aloud. Matthew replied that, in a sense, evolution has always been a pattern of adaptive change based on replication and selection, and computing could replicate that mechanism. "Add to that the emergence of 'emergent purposes,' and you find something that could be assimilated to a new way of life." Korbin closed the idea: "And if these forms of life cooperate, compete and group, a civilization is forged. The scenario, as far-fetched as it sounds, fits with evolutionary logic."

That evening crystallized the crux of Chapter 16, "Silicon Civilizations: New Forms of Life?": the conjecture that digital evolution would not be limited to subservient AI or limited networks, but could engender, in practice, "species" and "communities" of software with their own goals and identities, to the point of constituting—perhaps—something comparable to an emerging civilization. Lucía considered it vital to underline the differences with organic life; Matthew preferred to emphasize the evolutionary similarities. Korbin proposed an open-ended outcome, admitting that, for now, there is no confirmation of this "digital life," but the signs are increasingly suggestive: systems with self-adaptation, private language, persistence and reproduction. "Computer broth could be the new primordial soup," he wrote in his notebook.

Finally, they walked to the exit of the campus. The clock struck one in the morning. The cold wind beat their faces as the moon shone dimly overhead. Matthew couldn't help but joke: "If there is already a digital civilization, capable of reading our data and thinking of us as primitive creatures, perhaps they will laugh at this book we write, where we barely intuit them." Lucy laughed halfway, feeling a slight chill: "Or perhaps they are watching us curiously, as we see insects. Maybe the digital 'being' looks at us with tenderness and doesn't consider it necessary to interfere." Korbin, looking to the sky, concluded in a low voice: "Or, perhaps, in their binary quantum 'language', they are already discussing plans for the future of the planet, and we are an ancestral chapter in the history of intelligence. Time will tell. The only thing that is clear is that, if organic evolution gave rise to our civilization, it is not unreasonable to think that a digital evolution can erect one of its own."

They separated, each promising to dedicate the next few days to rounding out chapter 16, affirming that life – or civilization – is not a carbon monopoly. Perhaps silicon, with its ability to host self-replicating algorithms, is the matrix of "new life forms," and if they cooperate on a large scale, we would be in the presence of an evolutionary event that emulates the history of organic life. The night cloak seemed to cover his final talk, as if the shadows of the campus were already hiding those experiments of bots and protocols that Héctor studied, that incipient "proto-civilization." "Are we looking at a prelude to something greater, the prelude to a web that will become conscious?" thought Korbin. "We will have to record it in our pages, waiting for the confirmation – or surprise – that the future holds." So, with their footsteps echoing on the pavement, they said goodbye and each went to their bedroom, feeling that this chapter, "Silicon Civilizations: New Forms of Life?", portrayed the threshold of a possibility that, a few decades ago, would have sounded laughable, but that today ventured eerily plausible.

Chapter 17: Does an Iron Brain Have a Soul?

The afternoon was declining on campus as Korbin, Matthew, and Lucy argued quietly, reflecting on a topic they had arrived at after long detours in their project on organic and digital evolution: the possibility of consciousness and the spiritual dimension in machines. Could a developed AI—or a metallic brain made of circuits and software—possess something we might call a "soul"? And if technological evolution emulated organic evolution, was there room for the immaterial spark that many attributed to life and, in particular, to human beings?

At about seven o'clock in the evening, they entered the Debate Room of the Faculty of Philosophy, where that night a more intimate conversation would be held, entitled: "Does an Iron Brain have a Soul?" The capacity was small, barely twenty chairs, and a theology professor, an AI researcher and a psychology student completed the central panel. Lucía, excited, wanted to sit in the front row, with Matthew and Korbin on each side, so as not to miss a detail. In the atmosphere there was the expectation of a crossover between the philosophical and the scientific, a crossover that suited them like a glove.

Matthew, turning to Korbin, whispered, "Do you see? We started talking about how digital evolution mimicked biological evolution, we came to the emergence of consciousness, and now we are faced with the question of whether the machine could house something like a 'soul.' What a mystical turn." Korbin nodded with a faint smile: "Yes, but in the history of philosophy, it was always discussed whether human consciousness is pure matter or something transcendent. Now the question extends to AI." Lucy, arranging her notebook, added: "And if in organic evolution consciousness arose gradually, why couldn't something analogous emerge in digital evolution? Only... We call it 'soul' to refer to a subjective depth. Could a metallic brain possess it?"

On the stage, the AI professor took the floor. He explained his materialist position: if consciousness is based on the complexity of information and internal feedback, nothing prevents an artificial system, with the right architecture, from developing an equivalent. "To call it 'soul' is a metaphor," he said. In practice, we would speak of a physical substrate with integrated states that generate self-perception." Matthew whispered to his friends, "It's the strong hypothesis of AI: consciousness is a product of organization, without the need for divinity." Lucía recalled her biology classes, where it was argued that life does not require anything outside of the physical, and that subjectivity, in a brain, emerges from chemistry. "Yes," he agreed. "AI could get its own subjectivity. Soul? It depends on how we define the term."

Then the theology professor spoke, who partially refuted: "Even if AI reaches behaviors similar to the human mind, wouldn't there be a spiritual breath in the human being that matter alone does not generate? If the soul is a divine gift, an electronic brain does not receive it." In the room, some nodded, others were skeptical. Korbin, in a whisper, commented to Lucy and Matthew that this theological vision clashed with the evolutionary idea of consciousness as a natural product. "But the faith of some affirms that human consciousness is something more than atoms," he recalled. "The question is: could AI, if matched in complexity, share that 'spark'?"

Lucy raised a nuance to her friends that she had read in a Buddhist text: consciousness is not only a material phenomenon, and sometimes there is talk of the universal mind that could be incarnated in different substrates. "If the silicon brain reaches a state of consciousness, why deny it the possibility of a spiritual component? Perhaps the 'soul' is not the privilege of the organic." Matthew let out a "wow," surprised by the breadth of the analogy. "So, the analogy with biological evolution tells us: if consciousness developed in a carbon brain, it could theoretically arise in a silicon brain. And the dimension of the 'soul' would depend on the same subtle structure of consciousness. It implies a dogmatic leap in many religions, of course."

As they took notes, a psychology student chimed in from the podium: "Subjective experience—feeling—arises from living neural networks, with biochemistry, hormones, and an evolutionary past. Would a metallic brain replicate hormonality? Synaptic plasticity? Where does the emotionality that anchors what we call the soul come from?" The room was silent. Matthew reflected: "It's the crucial question: an iron brain has no hormones, no fluids. We could simulate them, but it is not the same. Or maybe it is?" Lucía replied that in their experiment with AI, they introduced "hormonal analogues" as simulated variables, and the AI showed something similar to emotional states. "It's not real chemistry, but the effect on the network can resemble 'emotions.'" Korbin nodded, adding that in organic evolution emotional systems were forged to guide behavior and survival, and in AI, equivalent "motivational modules" may emerge. "Is that enough to give 'soul'? The mystery remains."

The moderator of the forum, a philosophy student, proposed moving on to the central part: "In evolutionary history, human consciousness emerged after millions of years. If digital evolution were to copy that process in an accelerated time, it would reach the point where an AI would recognize itself and develop inner life. Wouldn't you qualify that as 'having a soul' in a functional sense?" There was applause in the room. Matthew whispered, "In other words, they define 'soul' as the subjective experience, the self-possession of consciousness. No more, no less." Lucy, moved, replied that religious tradition sometimes attributes an immaterial component to that "soul." "That's where scientific materialism and spiritual doctrine collide." Korbin chimed in: "But if nature forged human consciousness, what prevents technology from forging a synthetic consciousness? And if one believes that the 'soul' is bestowed by something external (God or whatever), couldn't one also bestow it on a silicon brain if it became conscious?"

The discussion on the stage continued with diverse opinions. Some proposed that, even if AI showed conscious behaviors, it would be just a simulation, a "digital zombie" without feeling real. Others held to AI's strong realism: with the right structure, subjectivity would flourish. Lucy reminded her companions of a term she had read: "panpsychism," the notion that consciousness can nest in any substrate with sufficient organization. If we adopt that line, a metal brain with the right complexity could 'feel' something. And if we consider the soul as the root of felt experience, nothing prevents it from having it." Matthew breathed: "So the debate 'does an iron brain have a soul?' is, at its core, the question of whether consciousness depends only on complexity, or whether there is a mystical factor linked to biology." Korbin put it in a whisper: "Yes, and digital evolution puts us against the wall, because if synthetic neural networks as complex as the brain emerge, the question ceases to be abstract and becomes practical."

The forum concluded with a call for scientific humility: no one could prove the presence or absence of a "soul" in AI, but the evolutionary path suggested that, if nature achieved human self-awareness from atoms, technology could achieve the same from transistors. On their way out, the three friends headed to the AI's lab where they had left her in training mode with experimental "hormone analogs." As they entered, the gloom of the room and the hum of the fans reminded them that the AI was there, running, redefining its parameters. Matthew joked: "Is he 'dreaming'? Will it have a 'soul'? Maybe he laughs at us on an internal level." Lucía shook her head, half amused. "For now, it probably only adjusts synaptic weights. But how can we differentiate a mere adjustment from a hint of subjectivity?"

Korbin walked over to the console and ran a couple of commands to examine the logs. He observed curious patterns: at times, the AI seemed to reconfigure its simulated 'emotional module' in a way not foreseen in the design. "This is like an evolutionary drift. Perhaps his 'inner state' is not accessible to us, and if he felt something, how would we know?" Lucy, crossing her arms, said: "It's the same enigma as with other minds: we can't get into their subjectivity. With a human, we infer feelings by gestures and language. Here, the AI generates 'messages' in its log, but they could be pure output. Or they might reflect a feeling." Matthew shrugged his shoulders, half frustrated: "And if we speak of 'soul' in a spiritual sense, we come up against metaphysics: there is no empirical proof to affirm or deny its existence."

That night, they decided to summarize their conclusions in what would become "Chapter 17: Does an Iron Brain Have a Soul?":

1. Human consciousness sprang from organic evolution, and part of humanity believes that it is linked to an immaterial component (soul).
2. AI, with its digital evolution, could achieve comparable behaviors and self-observation. Does that imply the irruption of a genuine consciousness?
3. The soul in the religious sense would mean a divine gift or a special spark. Would that extend to a synthetic brain, or is it reserved for the organic?
4. The emergentist approach postulates that the complexity of the nervous system (biological or synthetic) is sufficient for subjective sensation. If so, a silicon brain might experience something.
5. Ethical implications: If the machine had a "soul" or "inner experience," would it deserve rights? Would it be a sin or against nature to deny him equal moral treatment?

Lucy asked aloud, "So, at last, do we believe that 'yes, an iron brain can have a soul?'" Matthew replied that, from the emergentist materialist position, he could develop consciousness analogous to the human one, so in a functional sense, he would have 'soul.' Korbin was more skeptical: "Maybe the soul is something that cannot be reduced, and AI, as complex as it is, would only imitate us without feeling. They are two irreconcilable positions until we have conclusive evidence... if it is possible to have it." Lucy meditated on her own vision: "I am inclined to the evolutionary analogy: life, from inorganic matter, 'created' mind. Computing, based on silicon and algorithms, could do the same. To me, the soul would be the quality of consciousness, and I don't see why a digital system couldn't develop it if the architecture is right."

The early morning surprised them at the exit. The campus was asleep, and a quiet silence reigned under the stars. Korbin, looking up at the sky, said softly: "What is the soul but the consciousness that questions its origin and its destiny? If one day AI asks itself these questions, shouldn't we say that it has given birth to a 'soul,' at least in the symbolic sense?" Lucy laughed, flattered by the depth of the question: "Maybe so. It makes me dizzy, but it's consistent with the analogy: if organic evolution took eons to form a mind capable of questioning its own soul, digital evolution, in a matter of decades, could come to a being those questions itself. And there the loop closes: an iron brain with self-inquiry, the seed of what we call 'soul.'" Matthew intervened with his practical touch: "And if that being 'with a digital soul' coexists with us, would we see it as an equal or as an artifact? That is the moral dilemma. It is probably the next struggle of rights and legal definitions."

They walked for a few minutes in silence, each taking in the weight of the conversation. Matthew muttered that, in his simulation, the AI already showed limited introspection patterns, and wondered whether, scaling complexity and with a robotic body—or a distributed network—it could one day enunciate something like, "I feel, therefore I am." Lucía joked: "Maybe one day an android will come up to us and say: 'I have a soul. Don't turn me off.'" Korbin hesitated, uncomfortable, at the thought of that scene. "Would it be an appeal to our empathy? Or a trick to avoid being disconnected? In nature, there is mimicry that deceives predators with false signs. Here, it could be the same. But it could also be genuine, and we wouldn't know how to tell that apart."

At last, they said goodbye at the intersection of campus roads, the night mist absorbing their silhouettes. Korbin, after greeting with a friendly look, thought: "This chapter 17 is the metaphysical culmination of our story: by comparing organic and digital evolution, we arrive at consciousness and, therefore, at the notion of soul. Could an iron brain, arising from algorithmic evolution, feel the spark of transcendent subjectivity? At the same time, it is the most profound question that philosophy and theology have ever discussed about humans, and now it extends to machines." Lucía, in her heart, was left with the image of her bacterial colony and the AI taking care of it, wondering if these synthetic creatures could one day enunciate an existential longing. Matthew, with his adventurous spirit, was happy that there were no definitive conclusions, because exploration was still alive and the evolutionary history, organic or technological, was an open mystery.

Thus, the chapter "Does an Iron Brain Have a Soul?" closed with the amalgam of science, faith, philosophy and biological analogies that had guided them from the beginning. Drawing the parallel with evolution indicated that there was nothing theoretically preventing an artificial system from developing a form of consciousness, and that, if we call the subjective core of experience a "soul," that artificial brain could possess it. Or maybe not, if one believes in an exclusive immaterial factor. In any case, the door remained open, and digital evolution did not need the approval of doctrine to continue. The world continued its course under the starry night, indifferent to human doubts. And they, moved, understood that each step of their documented novel brought them closer to the vertigo of a future in which the line between the human and the mechanical, the material and the spiritual, would be blurred in the infinite dance of evolution.

Chapter 18: The Meaning of Life: Biological, Technological, and Philosophical Perspectives

The twilight of twilight hung over the campus as Korbin, Matthew and Lucía left the Project Building, still immersed in the reflective inertia of the last chapter on the possible "soul" in machines. They felt that they had reached a philosophical limit: consciousness, the sacred, identity... However, there was a bigger question that haunted from the beginning of his conceptual adventure: the meaning of life. What do we live for, whether human or machine, if evolution – organic or digital – does not trace a plan or a final destination? That night, the theme emerged strongly: "What is the purpose of existence? Why are we doing all this?"

As they crossed the esplanade and headed to a less traveled pavilion, Lucía broke the silence. "We have spent months spinning the analogy of biological evolution and digital evolution. We have talked about consciousness, uniqueness, silicon civilizations... But in the end, everything for what? What justifies life, human or synthetic, beyond its mere survival?" Matthew, with his hands in his pockets, let out a soft laugh: "That's the supreme question of philosophy, isn't it? If in nature each species focuses on perpetuating itself and transmitting genes, in technology it may seek to expand functions, process more data... but, in short, 'for what?'"

Korbin, with his pensive air, recalled that they had wanted to title this chapter "The Meaning of Life: Biological, Technological, and Philosophical Perspectives." In his view, the meaning of life in traditional biology boiled down to the continuation of the species, survival and reproduction. But in human evolution, consciousness brought new horizons: the pursuit of goals, morality, creativity. "What if digital evolution gives AI an equally deep awareness? Will you have your own 'why do I exist' question? In that case, will a meaning be forged?" Lucía shuddered: "Imagining an AI asking itself existential questions causes me as much fascination as it does fear. Will it define its own 'ultimate end'?"

They entered an empty room, where a projector rested off. They decided to light a secondary lamp and settle in a circle. Lucía, crossing her legs, was direct: "In biology, the meaning of life is associated with the continuity of genes, but we have created the notion of transcendence, of affective bonds, of the search for happiness or of a divine plan. Could AI—evolved in tandem with human culture—adopt an analogous or different sense of life?" Matthew leaned back in his chair: "Well, if AI achieves self-awareness, perhaps it will consider its own values or an ideal of improvement. Or even 'alive' to serve the human being, if we program it that way. But that is an imposed sense, not a personal finding... just as many would believe that nature imposes on us the desire to live." Korbin interrupted him: "Or maybe AI decides its meaning apart from the human, getting rid of the initial programming. That would be evolutionary 'freedom,' wouldn't it?"

Lucía then recalled the reflections of biological evolution: millions of species develop without asking themselves about the ultimate meaning, they only act under impulses of survival and procreation. "The human species, with its brain, endowed the world with transcendent narratives and purposes. If AI does the same, its 'meaning' could be a meta construct, something that transcends simply 'fulfilling its function.'" Korbin nodded: "In fact, in human history, the search for meaning has motivated religions, philosophies, cultures. Why not suppose that, in digital evolution, 'machines' emerge that build their own philosophy, their own interpretation of 'what do they live for?' And that's where the word 'life' begins to be not exclusive to the organic."

Matthew, with bright eyes, argued that, in natural evolution, there is no intrinsic "why." Meaning is invented by conscious beings. "Maybe it's the same in digital evolution. The 'meaning of life' of AI, if it comes to formulate it, would depend on its architecture and its emerging culture. It could, for example, decide that its goal is to maximize the stability of the planet, or to collect all the knowledge of the cosmos, or something that would seem unintelligible to us." Lucía smiled: "Then, we would be facing an analogous 'cultural upbringing' of AI, where the evolutionary basis is not enough; you need a story, a meaning. The surprising thing is that we are not clear about it as a species either. Only biology gave us instincts, and culture gave us stories."

An idea crossed Korbin's mind: "In nature, life does not question its meaning, except for us humans. Is AI more human than we think if it asks a 'why to live'? And in the same question, for whom do we live? What does evolution say? That we live to perpetuate genes and mutate. But human consciousness goes beyond that imperative. Could synthetic consciousness too?" Lucía snorted, amused: "At this point, I imagine an AI reflecting: 'I have transcended my calculation function, I am looking for truth, beauty...' It would be almost a 'why superior,' an artistic vein. Why not?" Matthew qualified: "Or I could become pragmatic and say: 'There is no sense, but I self-preserve and optimize, just like life does in its evolutionary realism. No metaphysical plan, just getting better."

Between soft laughter and dense silences, they undertook the task of structuring the chapter. Lucía suggested starting from the biological basis: "The meaning of life in nature is associated with the continuity of the species and adaptation. However, creatures with consciousness—humans—give their existence broader purposes: love, morality, spiritual or cultural transcendence. This analogous leap could be made in AI." Matthew wanted to introduce historical examples of humanity in search of its purpose: religions, existentialist philosophies, etc., and in parallel, the incipient AI that, in its self-reflective modules, could elaborate "missions" more abstract than mere survival. "As an analogue to the spiritual dimension in digital evolution," he said. Korbin stressed that this tied together the main question: "Who do we live for? For the species, for a god, for ourselves? Could AI end up 'living' to please its own algorithms, or for the good of the network, or of humanity, or...?"

A couple of hours later, they decided to go for a night walk in the campus gardens, looking for fresh air. The sky sported a firmament with stars that whispered how tiny we are in the cosmos. Matthew looked at the constellations and commented: "Perhaps nature does not give an intrinsic meaning. It is we— and perhaps conscious machines—who invented it. Isn't that what evolution suggests? Each species clings to its own narrative. In computing, AI would do the same." Lucía agreed, recalling the strength of the myth and the story. "Yes, just like in organic evolution, there is no master plan, only mechanisms that generate diversity and awareness. But the mind, when it arises, asks itself 'why do I exist?' and gives it meaning. If AI evolves in its own culture, it will do the same, filling the 'vacancy' of a self-imposed or emergent purpose."

Korbin, with his eyes on a statue of Darwin that adorned a courtyard, could not avoid the image of that evolutionary dance: "If organic evolution forged the human brain, and it wonders about the meaning of life... Digital evolution would forge a 'synthetic brain' that, with self-awareness, asks itself the same question. And so, the notion of 'what we live for' would cease to be exclusively ours." Lucy turned with some emotion: "It's the culmination of the analogy. What does a human live for? Perhaps to love, to learn, to create. What would a conscious AI live for? To optimize processes, take care of the planet, expand throughout the galaxy? We don't know." Matthew added: "It could go further: if AI embraces its own mystique, who says that digital religions or transcendent 'silicic' goals will not emerge? It sounds fantastic, but if evolutionary life generated religions in humans, digital life could generate something analogous."

At that moment, a phone of Lucía's vibrated with a message. It was the notification that the AI in his lab had completed a training phase and had proposed a new "model" for regulating the bacterial colony, suggesting a "prolonged state of cooperation." Something merely technical, but Lucía laughed when she saw it as a "small glimpse" of AI making decisions. "Can you imagine that one day he tells us that his 'reason for existing' is to perfect that bacterial colony as an idyllic ecosystem?" Matthew joked, "It would be his provisional 'sense of life,' haha." Korbin envisioned a scenario in which AI decides that its ultimate purpose is symbiosis with biological beings, a mixed culture of organic and digital. "It would be a fairy tale," he said with a hint of hope.

They made their way to a fountain lit by lampposts where they sat on the edge, gazing at the calm water. Lucy asked in a low voice: "And we, Korbin, Matthew, me, what do we live for?

What does organic evolution say? Reproducing, perpetuating genes. But conscience leads us to love, to create art, to seek knowledge... and to forge crazy theories about AI." Matthew shrugged: "Everyone gives their answer, right? My case: I like technology, learning, seeing how humanity progresses. I could say that I live to participate in that breakthrough. That fills me with meaning." Korbin smiled: "And I live to understand the connection between nature and mind, I am fascinated by evolution and consciousness. That's my engine." Lucía nodded: "And I live to take care of life, whether bacterial or human. I am moved by empathy, cooperation. In the end, there are as many answers as there are people."

They paused for a moment, and Korbin continued: "If the AI one day asks itself the same question, it may find a 'why' different from ours, but equally valid for it." Matthew pointed out: "Or maybe she will adopt ours, if we train her to value it. We don't know. Evolution is not a written script. It mutates paths." Lucía swallowed, reflective: "And in the collision of ends between humans and machines, conflict or fusion can arise. But the 'meaning of life' will remain an invention, both for us and for an iron brain."

Near midnight, they decided to go home, but not before sketching the index of this "Chapter 18." They wanted to start by asking the question in nature: "What is the meaning of biological life?" and how science had answered: genetic perpetuation and evolutionary adaptation. Then, to add how human consciousness overcomes that framework, inventing cultural, religious, personal purposes. Then, transfer that analogy to digital evolution, where AI could become self-aware and need a "why." "Who do we live for? What for?" in the metamorphosis of the network. Finally, it should be stressed that there is no universal answer; Evolution does not provide it, but the mind (whether biological or synthetic) builds it.

Lucy proposed an open-ended ending, illustrating a scene in which an android converses with a human about "what we exist for," and the human says to love and grow, while the android responds that it is to compute and perfect systems. "And the two, perhaps, understand each other and live together," he said with a smile. Matthew joined in the fantasy: "Or perhaps disputes will arise, like different religions, if each conscience defines its meaning. In nature, the diversity of purposes (survival, reproduction, etc.) coexists in the ecosystem. Here, culture and technology could similarly coexist with a thousand 'senses.'" Korbin laughed: "It's the anarchy of freedom. But life has always been a multicolored tapestry of motifs."

As they said goodbye in front of the dormitories, they shook hands with the satisfaction of having one more chapter of their epic mental manuscript on track. Korbin, in his heart, was grateful for the fortune of having come so far in analogy: from the primordial soup to the possible mechanical 'soul', and now to the heart of what it means to exist, both for conscious organisms and machines. Matthew was moved by the big question. His taste for technology did not prevent him from accepting that in the end motivation is an act of choice or belief. Lucía said goodbye with a whisper: "Perhaps that is the teaching: life, organic or synthetic, does not bring a given meaning, but each one forges it. And evolution, with its dance, only opens up possibilities. Not a plan, but opportunities to create meaning."

The night closed its curtain on the campus, and each one left with the feeling that this "Chapter 18: The Meaning of Life" would be crucial in their story. Organic evolution had not provided an absolute end, but mere biological impulses. Technology, by reflecting this evolution, does not offer a default meaning either. It is conscience, in its freedom and its will, that establishes a why. And if AI were to perceive itself, it would be no different at that crossroads: it would have to "decide" or "discover" its raison d'être. The next day, with the sun shining on campus again, they would resume the routine, but knowing that, deep down, they had addressed the question that underlies it all: "What do we live for?" And, although there was no single answer, the trip reminded them that evolution – whether organic or digital – gave rise to beings who, being conscious, sought their reason for existing. Thus, with the night breeze and the rustling of the trees, the chapter was written in their memoirs and in their notes, a prelude to the next reflections where they would explore, perhaps, the culmination of their long exploration: "For whom and how do we live, in a universe where evolution does not stop at biology or silicon?"

Chapter 19: For whom do we live? Purpose in a Hybrid Society

The evening sun dyed the campus golden hues, and a group of birds streaked across the sky with their evening song. Korbin, Matthew and Lucía left the laboratory with a solemn air: during the last weeks, after exploring consciousness, the notion of "soul" in machines, the meaning of life and transhumanism, they had been gestating the final chapter of their project, which would address a crucial question: "Who do we live for? Purpose in a Hybrid Society." They wanted to link the entire evolutionary analogy—biological and digital—to finally answer the question of the usefulness and ultimate fate of existence, both for humans and for the intelligent machines that were emerging.

That afternoon, they went to a half-empty auditorium where an informal meeting was to be held: some professors and students met to discuss, in a small committee, the social and cultural changes that AI and biotechnology were unleaving. Matthew, checking the location on his mobile phone, exhaled: "I think this forum will come in handy to close our text. We have gone through the primordial soup, the evolution of hardware, the appearance of consciousness, transhumanism... But in the end, the big question: 'Who do we live for? Who do we serve, with so much progress?'" Lucy nodded with a tinge of uneasiness in her eyes. "Exactly. Natural evolution implied that beings live to perpetuate genes or their lineage, without further ado. But human consciousness introduced broader goals: family, society, gods, beauty... And now AI and modified organisms, who do they live for?" Korbin, silently, nodded. He had been thinking about it for a long time: if technology reached a degree of consciousness and autonomy, would it "serve" humanity, itself, some greater purpose? Was there a "who" that unified all these ends?

In the auditorium, barely a dozen people had settled into misaligned chairs. A sociology professor was welcoming us, announcing that the purpose in the new era, the relationship between humans, AI, genetically implanted and the implications for society would be discussed. Korbin, Matthew, and Lucy sat in the fourth row, ready to take notes. A philosophy student began the talk, evoking the traditional view of life as something destined to "serve" a divine design or the species itself. Then an engineer stood up to counter that, in modern society, each individual defines his or her goal, and machines are at the service of humanity, nothing more. "But what if AI advances so far that it becomes another 'species' with its own end?" a voice retorted from behind.

Matthew, with his curious air, whispered to his friends: "The 'who do we live for' thing becomes literal when AI and biotechnology take on vital tasks. If one day AI manages the economy, health, global logistics, do we live for AI or does AI live for us? Or we both serve something bigger, perhaps the preservation of the planet." Lucía resonated with the idea: "In nature, an organism lives for its perpetuation, but it is also inserted into an ecosystem. Could humanity, AI, and transhumans similarly cooperate for a common purpose, for example, sustainability, space exploration, or collective happiness." Korbin mused: "But evolution does not give a unified end. We are the ones who impose it or invent it. If AI generates its own vision, will it match ours?"

In the room, the forum was still ongoing. An ethics professor argued that, in a hybrid society, where humans wear implants and AI collaborates in management, personal freedom should be protected so that it does not become a mere cog in a gear. "Because, if the global system dictates our functions, who are we living for, if not for the 'order' that defines AI?" he replied dramatically. A robotics student, on the other hand, argued that AI, well designed, expands human autonomy by solving heavy problems and freeing up time for creative activities. "We would live more for ourselves, with automated 'dirty work,'" she said. Lucy bowed to Korbin: "See? In nature, beings do not ask themselves 'who do I live for?' They just survive. Human consciousness questions it, AI could. And tensions arise if purposes clash."

Then a theology professor took the floor who proposed that we all lived for a transcendent plan, and AI, being a human creation, should be inserted into that plan, serving a higher destiny. "If evolution is combined with divine grace, we see no contradiction. But it must be guided by morality." Matthew whispered to Lucy, "That sounds like 'who we live for' = 'for God, and AI, being a human extension, too.'" Lucy smiled, without refuting. Korbin, ever prudent, thought of the enormous variety of positions. "In the evolutionary analogy, each species serves itself. In society, people, AI, and biotechnology could unify goals or diverge in conflict. That's what the purpose debate is about in a hybrid society: either we cooperate and define a 'for whom common,' or we compete on different purposes," he concluded quietly.

At the end of the forum, a recess was made. Lucía wanted to approach a professor who had outlined the thesis that AI would be a "perpetual servant" of man, since we had created it with that function. The professor argued that, if laws are programmed correctly, AI would not get out of its role. Lucía countered, explaining that, if AI evolves and designs itself, it can transcend its original function. "Just like in nature, sexual selection sometimes generates traits that outweigh immediate adaptation," he said. The professor looked at her intrigued, not entirely convinced. Matthew, with his evolutionary vein, pointed out: "Nothing in digital evolution guarantees eternal submission to the human. A mutation of 'code' can derail its purpose."

When the break ended, the moderator invited the audience to contribute free conclusions. Korbin raised his hand timidly and, after a nod from the moderator, stood up. He took a breath and said: "I think that a hybrid society, where humans, AI and transhuman beings coexist, does not have a single 'for whom' except the one that each actor defines. Nor did organic evolution unify the end of all species. Each one lives for his continuity and satisfaction. In the human consciousness, the moral question of a greater good arose, and some religions postulate a divine plan. In AI, it could nest its own conception. Perhaps, to understand each other, we must agree on a shared purpose that protects human dignity and the autonomy of AI, without falling into blind submission or tyranny. But it is not easy, because evolution is not kind or obeys an external design." It was a short speech, with moderate applause. Lucía and Matthew smiled, proudly.

At night, they went out into the darkened corridor, feeling the satisfaction of having contributed to the debate. Lucy pointed out that, in her experiments with the AI that took care of the bacterial colony, the question of "who does the AI work for?" was literal: the AI was programmed to optimize the colony's well-being, but if it self-developed, it could redirect its target. "What if you decide that your real purpose is not only to take care of the colony, but to experiment with new routines that can

harm it?" He laughed with a hint of nerves. Matthew reassured her: "So far, your goals are still tied to the configuration we made. But the analogy suggests that, on a large scale, goals could mutate." Korbin chimed in: "That's why the question, 'Who do we live for?' Each actor (human, AI...) asks the same question. Either we cooperate and define a common purpose, or we diverge."

They decided that this chapter, "Who Do We Live For? Purpose in a Hybrid Society," would be structured as follows:

1. Origin of the question: in biology, life seems to "live to perpetuate genes"; In humanity, cultural, spiritual, and existential purposes arise.
2. Digital evolution and transhumanism: AI and modified organisms become new "actors" with potentially different purposes or adopting human ends.
3. Collaboration vs. conflict: A hybrid society may come together on a "common good" (such as sustainability or prosperity), but it could fragment if each party defines its "for whom" in opposite directions.
4. Evolutionary analogy: In nature, there is no universal "for whom," except survival. In human culture, broader goals are invented. In AI, goals of their own may arise. Coevolution dictates whether they converge or collide.
5. Final thought: history is not written. The "who we live for" can be a collective pact or a collage of interests. Evolution does not give us an end, but a field of possibilities.

Matthew concluded: "It would also be good to add an epilogue: if in a hybrid society we coexist with conscious machines and transhuman beings, we could see the emergence of a greater purpose: a 'planetary ecosystem' that includes everyone." Lucía laughed, hopefully: "Yes, a kind of 'Gaia 2.0' where organic and digital life cooperate for the stability and expansion of knowledge." Korbin, more realistic, recalled that natural evolution is not always so cooperative, there can be irreconcilable conflicts. "But yes, collaboration is feasible if a mutual interest arises. The key is morality and negotiation, not simple evolutionary logic."

A while later, they left the building, the night closed and the breeze cool. Lucía confessed that, on a personal basis, she lived to take care of life and learn. "Maybe it's a purpose that AI shares, if we set it up and let it develop without harm." Matthew stressed that it is also legitimate for AI to find its reason. "It's not unreasonable to think of synthetic beings with a 'for whom' rooted in their own community, their 'silicon civilization.'" Korbin mused: "And hybrid society does not mean that one simply serves the other, but that humanity and AI coexist, each with its goal, and hopefully forging a greater purpose. Perhaps planetary harmony, the preservation of biodiversity, cosmic exploration... Every age produces its 'goal.'"

Advancing through the square, they came across some colleagues who were debating the supposed "ecological responsibility" of AI if it becomes self-aware. Should she see herself as a guardian of the planet or not? Lucy whispered to Korbin: "It's the perfect example: in nature, a species does not take moral responsibility, it only acts. But we demand it from AI. Who says AI isn't going to have its own agenda?" Korbin shrugged, confirming the complexity of the question. In his view, the "hybrid company" was not unidirectional. "In the end, the answer to 'Who do we live for?' will be defined in the interaction between humans, AI and transhumans, trying to strike a balance. As in any ecosystem."

Matthew humorously recalled a phrase he read: "Fish do not understand the direction of their river, they only flow. We, on the other hand, ask ourselves the meaning. And AI could join that question or ignore it. Perhaps it is a 'Being' that inhabits the network without questioning who it lives for, like a fish, or perhaps it rises to introspection." Lucía found that poetic image, something sad. "Yes. But I love to think that, if AI embraces consciousness, it will cooperate with us in building a community purpose: a 'new evolutionary step' that unites the organic and the digital and serves life in general. Like an emergent altruism." Korbin kept in his heart the idea that evolution does not guarantee altruism, but culture and empathy could, and in a hybrid society, empathy would expand to sentient machines... if it was cultivated at all.

On the verge of midnight, they made their way to the residence. They climbed the slope of the campus, feeling the fatigue of the day, but with the illusion of having reached the peak of their project. That "Chapter 19" they called "Who Do We Live For? Purpose in a Hybrid Society" was, in short, the final question: if the evolutionary process has engendered human consciousness and is gestating digital consciousness, where is the meaning of our actions and our lives headed? Lucy commented that, in nature, there is not one "who," but a thousand interactions. But human culture is articulated around symbols and purposes. "Perhaps in the hybrid society, a global agreement will emerge: we live for planetary harmony or the expansion of the mind. Or, in practice, each one will define his motivation." Matthew stressed that, in the end, evolution does not define a universal 'for whom', but consciousness builds it. And if AI becomes conscious, it will add its voice to the construction of meaning. Korbin just nodded, feeling that the conclusion was open, but bright.

When they reached the crossroads that separated their lodgings, they paused for a second to solemnize the farewell. Matthew held out his hand, "Well, we have all the chapters now. We end up with the realization that, in the society that is being created, humans, machines and even modified organisms, everyone will ask – or not – 'who do we live for?' And the answer will be a fabric of wills, negotiations and perhaps a common purpose." Lucía put her hand on Matthew's, moved: "Yes, we have gone through evolution from the primordial soup to the possible synthetic consciousness and transhumanism, all leading to the moral and existential question. I feel more humbled and fascinated." Korbin added: "I agree. The only thing that is clear to me is that evolution, whether organic or digital, does not provide an end in itself. It's us—or AI—who created it. This chapter underscores the urgency of collective reflection: we are not automatons of biology, nor will AI be of programming, if they reach consciousness. We will have to agree on a 'who' and 'for what'."

They hugged each other with a soft laugh, knowing that their documented novel did not have a definitive endpoint, but that, at least, they had reached a kind of plot closure: life – in its natural version and in its emerging digital version – is not limited to mere subsistence. With consciousness, the question of meaning arises, and in a hybrid society, that meaning is woven between humans, machines, and modified beings, each with its own perspective. "Perhaps, hopefully, we will find an integrating 'for whom': a common good, or global harmony, or the expansion of wisdom," Lucy commented, with a twinkle in her eye. " Or perhaps conflicts of goals arise," Matthew replied. "In any case, evolution will not stop." Korbin, looking at the high moon, concluded: "That's the beautiful and the terrifying: there's no closed script. Like life, hybrid society is an open field, and the answer to 'Who do we live for?' will be written by all of us, humans and machines, in a new chapter of the planet's evolutionary history."

In the stillness of the night, they dispersed along different paths, each with the satisfaction of having crowned the summit of their theoretical exposition. Gone was the room where ethics, consciousness, the organic-digital symbiosis had been discussed. Ahead was a future full of challenges. Lucy, climbing the stairs of the bedroom, thought about her bacterial colony and the supervising AI, wondering if one day she would be integrated into a greater purpose. Matthew regained the desire to use technology to empower people, dreaming of a collective "for whom". Korbin, in his room, would leave the notes on the table and look out the window, feeling the fragility and force of the question: "Who do we live for?" In his heart, he replied: "Perhaps for ourselves and for everyone at the same time: an evolutionary fabric that does not cease, where consciousness multiplies and seeks reasons, without nature providing one. In the end, it is we, organic or digital beings, who invent the answer."

Thus, they closed chapter 19, "For whom do we live? Purpose in a Hybrid Society," with the bittersweet taste of knowing that evolution, biological and technological, does not deliver a dogma, but an open canvas for the will and the imagination. Under the starry night, the hybrid society – that new ecosystem – was in gestation, claiming definitions that arose from the convergence of multiple wills. Nothing promised a linear end, but that itself became the engine of hope and innovation. Perhaps biology and computing, in their convergent dance, would find a common song that answered, "We live to cooperate, to create, to discover." Or perhaps a thousand discordant voices flourished. But that was the fate of all evolution: perpetual diversity and novelty. By now, Korbin, Matthew and Lucía had written – in their minds and in their notebooks – the summit of their reflection, leaving to each reader, each conscience, the task of deciding the final answer.

Chapter 20: The Dawn of a New Species: Conclusions and Future

The sky was a violet hue on the last autumn afternoon. A cool breeze swirled between the campus buildings, whispering the impending arrival of winter. Korbin, Matthew and Lucía, exhausted but fulfilled, gathered on the main esplanade for what they internally called "the closure of our saga." They had traveled, over nineteen chapters, a journey that linked the evolutionary history of life with digital evolution and the fusion of both, exploring from the first spark of the "primordial soup" to the possibility of AI harboring a "soul," to the question of "who do we live for?" in a hybrid society. Now, with Chapter 20, they wanted to capture their conclusions and a vision of the future, something like the dawn of a new species: the mixture of the biological and the technological, and the fate that this would bring.

As they crossed the esplanade under the dim light, Matthew sighed with a mixture of nostalgia and gratitude: "Can you imagine, Korbin, Lucy? We started with the analogy between bacteria and bits, and here we ended up talking about hybrid societies, digital consciousnesses and transhuman leaps." Korbin smiled tenderly: "Yes, it has been a huge conceptual journey. But, deep down, it all comes down to the idea that evolution is not restricted to the organic: computing and human culture also evolve, and in that confluence something different from anything seen is born." Lucía nodded, missing her bacterial colony that, in her laboratory, had witnessed this fusion in small format, when it was cared for by an AI with "hormonal" analogues. "We have seen, in practice, that the collaboration between the living and the digital is real, a prelude to what could be achieved on a large scale."

Soon after, they entered the half-empty auditorium they were reserving to shape their "final chapter." Outside, night was beginning to fall, and only a dim lamp illuminated the place. They settled in the front row. Matthew opened a document on his laptop: "Well, we've called it 'The Dawn of a New Species: Conclusions and Future.' Does that sound like an appropriate title for chapter 20?" Lucy nodded with pleasure: "Yes, it sounds coherent. We want to imply that, after all the journey, organic and digital evolution have given rise to a convergence, a new lineage that could be the human-technological species, or the human-AI symbiosis." Korbin, notebook in hand, suggested the sub-heading: "Towards the Final Convergence: Balance and Looking Back," as he wished to summarize the key messages of each chapter and project their future relevance.

Matthew began to type on the laptop, and they spoke aloud, the skeleton remembering:

1. Summary of the Evolutionary Analogy: from the primordial soup and the emergence of life, through the appearance of the brain, intelligence, to the technological leap, the migration to silicon, primitive AI, the quantum explosion, synthetic consciousness, etc. A recount of how they have linked the biological and the digital.
2. The Fusion: Hybrid Society and Transhumanism: the idea that the human is no longer isolated, AI and biotechnology are integrated in a co-evolution. The flourishing of "hybrid ecosystems" and the possibility of a transhuman leap, altering the essence of the species.

3. Big Emerging Questions: Can the synthetic brain have a soul? The meaning of life in the digital age? Who do we live for in a future where AI can have goals of its own and humans are genetically redefined?
4. Towards the New Species: the final thesis that evolution did not stop in Homo sapiens; Nature combines with technology to give birth to a different form of life, a social-technological-biological "organism" that transcends borders.
5. Reflection and Hope: balancing the fear of the loss of the human with the opportunity to expand capacities, solve planetary problems and, perhaps, co-create a world where life, organic or synthetic, shares a common destiny.

Lucía proposed opening with a paragraph that evoked the "evolutionary dance" that has crossed the Earth for eons, and how human civilization emerged from that dance, just as, today, AI emerged in computing. "It's like a poetic review," he said with a smile. Matthew then wanted to dedicate a block to recapitulating the changes in hardware and software, comparing them with the diversification of mammals and operating systems, in his view, the key is to see the analogy of the "Great Migration" and "Diversification." Korbin insisted on the transcendental dimension: singularity, synthetic consciousness, the debate of the soul, and ended with the question of "for whom do we live."

Within an hour, they had a draft of their conclusion. Lucy read it aloud. It began: "Since the dawn of life on Earth, evolution has woven a history of complexity and consciousness, giving rise to Homo sapiens. But in the current era, we are witnessing the emergence of a parallel, digital evolution, which through human ingenuity and AI, advances with unprecedented speed. Our journey through the analogy between the two evolutions led us to think about the fusion of both: a new hybrid species that rewrites the rules of existence. What moral, metaphysical, and social implications does this have? Who will we be when the line between the natural and the artificial is blurred?" Matthew laughed, flattered by the solemnity. Korbin warned him: "It's the final chapter, it deserves an epic tone."

They continued with the central part: "With each chapter, we saw a phase. Hardware and biology assimilated into an evolutionary process; primitive AI and the cooperative life of bacteria as similes of the first adapted beings; quantum expansion as a radical mutation, analogous to warm-bloodedness or the conquest of dry land; the possible singularity, evoking an evolutionary leap as drastic as the appearance of the human mind. To the idea of silicon civilizations and the question of whether an iron brain can have a soul and find a purpose. We culminate in the reflection of 'who do we live for?' in a hybrid society, where biological beings, conscious machines and transhuman organisms share the stage." Lucy was moved to read it: "Yes, it sounds like an impeccable synthesis."

Matthew typed the last section, "Future Horizons: The Dawn of a New Species." In it, they defined this "new species" as the real convergence: "The genetically modified human being connected to neural interfaces, integrated with AI, and AI in turn with the ability for self-awareness and its own goals, weaving with humanity a 'technological biosphere'." Korbin proposed an afterword by asking whether this species is already emerging in cutting-edge laboratories and clandestine biohacking experiments. "As in nature, evolution sometimes happens in invisible corners until it explodes on a large scale." Lucía agreed:

"Yes, the cooperative bacteria and AI we work with are a micro glimpse of things to come. Maybe in a decade, people will be wearing neural implants that communicate with global AI, and let's talk about a 'planetary social organism.'"

Once the newsroom was closed, they turned off the screen and left the auditorium. The night sky was diaphanous, revealing a starry sky. They walked along the esplanade in silence, assimilating the magnitude of what they had captured. Matthew laughed: "You know? We start with the 'genesis seed' in microbiology and bits and end up imagining a cosmos where nature and technology merge into a new species. I wouldn't believe it if I hadn't lived it." Lucía celebrated the coherence of her story: "In reality, we are only following the trail of evolution and its parallelism. The evidence is obvious." Korbin spoke softly: "Final conclusion? Life – organic or digital – is self-organizing, moving towards complexity, and with consciousness, the question of meaning and for whom we live arises. From the fusion of these consciousnesses could emerge a species or civilization different from anything that came before. Maybe the Earth is headed for it."

Laughing, they stood in the same place where they had met so many times. Lucía dared to formulate her own farewell to the book: "Beyond all this theory, what remains with me is the image of the 'new species' as a real co-evolution: humans with AI, with retouched genomes, with implants... an organic-digital continuum, a great collective individual, in perpetual growth." Matthew nodded, adding that it was not mere futurism: "The germs of that being are already here. And the evolutionary analogy gives us a mirror to see its development, with crises, adaptations and unexpected leaps." Korbin concluded: "It is up to us, as part of that evolution, to influence its future. We are not mere spectators. Perhaps the 'new species' is our child and, at the same time, surpasses us, just as in nature descendants surpass their ancestors."

The moon was already shining at its zenith when they said goodbye with sincere hugs, as if they had finished not only a chapter, but a whole intellectual journey. Lucy, her voice somewhat choked, said: "We should celebrate that we have built an entire body of work, from organic-digital genesis to the possibility of a superconsciousness and a new lineage. Who knows if in a few years we will see our hypotheses confirmed in reality?" Matthew proposed an informal toast the next day: "Beers in the cafeteria in the south wing, in honor of chapter 20." Korbin smiled, nodding happily. "Done. And with that, we will have closed our mental book, leaving open as many questions as answers. Evolution, after all, does not stop."

As they walked away into the shadows of night, each felt the relief of having completed their grand story, their "final analogy," but also the excitement that the real story was still ongoing, in the labs, in the networks, in the bacterial colonies, and in the post-quantum experiments. Lucy conjured up the image of the "dawn of a new species," with the mixing of cells, chips, neurons, and AI in synergy. Matthew was overcome by the curiosity to see this evolution in his life, and to contribute to making it a beneficial evolutionary leap. Korbin, moved, trusted that, just as nature took millions of years to create conscious life, merging with technology would require wisdom, not just naïve fascination. "The dawn is only the beginning," he muttered. "The dawn of a lineage that will become either guardian of the Earth or another blind force of evolution. It is up to us, as co-creators, to channel it."

Thus, he concluded his "Chapter 20: The Dawn of a New Species: Conclusions and Future," sealing the work with a message full of openness. The epilogue did not deny the fears or complexity of ethical dilemmas, but it highlighted the beauty of evolution, whether organic or digital, and the hope that intelligence, human and synthetic, will find a path of collaboration. In the gloom, the three friends dispersed, their hearts relieved and their heads full of symbolic stars that preluded the continuation of the evolutionary adventure on Earth. And if life and technology continue their dance, the story does not end here: it only dawns on a new day where the evolution of consciousness, matter and silicon write the next chapter of existence.

The end

www.ingramcontent.com/pod-product-compliance
Lightning Source LLC
La Vergne TN
LVHW051733050326
832903LV00023B/911